THEOLOGICAL
REFLECTION
ON
DOROTHY DAY, PETER MAURIN
AND
THE CATHOLIC WORKER

ALL THE WAY TO

HEAVEN

BY LAWRENCE HOLBEN
FORWARD BY KATE CHATFIELD

WIPF & STOCK · Eugene, Oregon

Wipf and Stock Publishers
199 W 8th Ave, Suite 3
Eugene, OR 97401

All the Way to Heaven
A Theological Reflection on Dorothy Day, Peter Maurin and the Catholic Worker
By Holben, Lawrence
Copyright©1997 by Los Angeles Catholic Worker Community
ISBN 13: 978-1-60899-050-4
Publication date 4/29/2010
Previously published by Rose Hill Books Catholic Worker, 1997

Contents

Foreword

The reign of God is like a buried treasure which a man found in a field. He hid it again, and rejoicing at his find, went and sold all that he had and bought that field. Or again, the kingdom of heaven is like a merchant's search for fine pearls. When he found one really valuable pearl, he went back and put up for sale all that he had and bought it.
— Matthew 13:44-46

Catholic Workers live in an odd world. They live exposed to all the brokenness of this world — the poverty, addictions, despair, injustice, and violence — while proclaiming that the Kingdom of God is here. The Catholic Workers who have lived in houses of hospitality and on farms and who have fed the hungry, cared for the dying, been arrested, healed the land, and soothed the angry remain in the midst of all the brokenness, the broken Body of Christ, because they have found joy. They are the farmer and the merchant who have spied the treasure that is the Reign of God. Nothing can compare to the joy at finding that treasure, to finding the way to heaven that is heaven. There is joy in work that is meaningful, that is rooted in the Gospels, work on which no price is placed, not measured in an hourly wage or monthly salary, work that is integrated with one's most deeply held beliefs and values. This is holy work, and to encounter people who have been at this work for most of their lives is to meet holy people, with all their faults and contradictions, who inspire us to continue on the way.

I am not such a person, but I can attest to their existence. I have met many in person and in writing in my brief years as a Catholic Worker. I first came to the Catholic Worker in Los Angeles on a Wednesday night for a liturgy and potluck, with members of the community and visitors serving soup on the streets of Skid Row. At the time, I

worked at a non-profit agency on Skid Row, so I was somewhat fa-
miliar with the people and area, but being downtown with Catholic
Workers was a profoundly different experience. For though we had
the food to give, we were serving people where they lived; we were
coming to them rather than having them come to us, an approach that
was fundamentally different from the approach of other "service pro-
viders." At my job at a "homeless assistance agency," I worked behind a desk in a very controlled environment where the power relationship was very clearly established between me — the case manager
— and my homeless clients. Being on Skid Row at night, the power
relationship between us (the servants) and the served was shifted. If
violence erupted, community members would attempt to intervene to
prevent one person from hurting another, but nobody could be ordered
outside (we were already there), no doors could be barred (there were
none), and everybody would be welcome the next day at the dining
garden or the following Wednesday night. Having little else besides
the protection of one another and of God, we were attempting ser-
vanthood by relying on the benevolence and good will of those we
served.

In fact, it seemed that the very meaning of the word "service" was
being restored, the kind of service that put one at the mercy of the
served. A second difference I immediately noticed, and one which be-
lies the afore-mentioned threat of violence, was the friendliness that
existed between the community members and the people on the street.
Hugs were exchanged, as were jokes and mocking insults. All regu-
lars were called by their street names, and after the line dwindled, relaxed conversations took place. There was a level of respect that existed between the servants and the served that I had never before wit-
nessed. In retrospect it may have been the first time I'd ever seen the
Gospel so consciously attempted. It was the end of this first night that
I decided my next "job" would be at the Los Angeles Catholic
Worker. I had found a fine pearl.

It was wonderful work but it was exhausting. As a community, we
prayed together every day, and every day I prayed for strength. A not
unusual day could entail returning to the house after long hours serving at the dining garden only to be greeted by a loud schizophrenic
woman who needed me to take her to cash a check so that we could
go to the store to buy ingredients for Beef Stroganoff. Or, I would be
needed that night to sleep in the room of a dying guest or at the
kitchen, in order that it wouldn't get broken into yet again. One could

easily succumb to feelings of self-pity. There was always the sense that one was not appreciated, either by fellow community members or by those we served. Life outside the Catholic Worker seemed so much easier, where one clocked out at 5:00 p.m. and was shown appreciation in the form of a paycheck, if by nothing else. The ideals of the Catholic Worker were still inspiring but the daily reality of living in a house of hospitality seemed too much for me. In the eyes of the world, and increasingly in my eyes, it didn't seem that we were doing anything for the poor. We weren't "transitioning" anyone out of poverty, and we certainly weren't changing the structures of the world. One could easily feel frustrated in a house where "successful" hospitality meant that someone had died peacefully.

At the end of two years there, I gathered with members of my community and other Catholic Worker communities in southern California for a retreat. The speaker was Larry Holben who spoke on the theology of the movement — why we do what we do and how we are to do it. I remembered something Dan Berrigan had said about William Stringfellow: "He gave us the theology that lay behind our resistance actions. We [Berrigans and others] were acting instinctually in response to the Vietnam War and later, the nuclear weapons buildup, but Stringfellow was able to tell us, in biblical terms, what we were doing, why, and named for us who we were up against — the worldly powers and principalities." This is precisely what Larry gave to us in his talks, formal and informal, through the years. Many Workers were like me, instinctually drawn to the work and prayer, but without a clear understanding of why we were living this way. Larry's talks gave a starting point for that understanding: Every person we encountered, no matter how dirty, smelly, crazy, no matter how far from curing an addiction, or getting a job, was the center of God's saving plan for the world. And, as such, that person demanded our love and respect. This is why it didn't matter if we ever solved any social ill, served a thousand meals, or served one. My assistance in the Beef Stroganoff project of a mentally ill woman was one of a million results of Dorothy and Peter's project, which was rooted in Catholic social teaching and which drew all of its power from the Gospel message of radical love for one another. With such a precedence for my actions, how could I care for such worldly aims as effectiveness, or for a paycheck, or for where all this would lead me?

However, this theology would be hollow if it were meant only for those living in a Catholic Worker house, the same as insisting that the gospel is only for those who take religious vows, or that Christianity begins and ends at the church on Sundays. The message of the gospel is meant for all people and the beliefs and values of the Catholic Worker were never meant to begin and end at the walls of an "official" House of Hospitality. If one can only be a personalist or attempt to live the radical gospel message of love within the confines of a Catholic Worker house, then Peter Maurin's vision is a small one. But the challenge of Peter's vision is that we are called to live as Catholic Workers. As Christians, we are all called to perform the Corporal and Spiritual Works of Mercy at a personal cost. We are all called to be peacemakers. We are all called to live lives of voluntary poverty. We are all called to build a new world within the shell of the old and to serve God by serving the common good. A House of Hospitality is but one manifestation of this call to all Christians — something which Dorothy and Peter recognized as they preached the personalist message in person and in print. Just so, this book is not only for those in and around Catholic Worker Houses of Hospitality, but also reminds all of us of the way we are called to lead our lives — the way that is heaven. And, in living this way, don't be surprised if you find joy.

> — *Kate Chatfield*
> *Kieran Prather House*
> *San Bruno Catholic Worker*

Introduction

I first encountered the Catholic Worker movement in the summer of 1976, at a point of significant personal transition and flux in my own life. Having experienced some limited early success as a screenwriter, the larger achievements to which I aspired nevertheless seemed to elude me — I was at the time ghost-writing the autobiography of a mass murderer. My wife and I had recently separated. I was spending considerable energy attempting to build a life of sophistication and tasteful acquisition that I hoped would somehow expunge the stain of a narrow, lower middle-class fundamentalist upbringing.

Having decided — not without cause — that my life was "too selfish," I asked a socially-conscious friend where she thought I might do volunteer work. A week or so later I was driving my chartreuse Karmann Ghia convertible up to the Gladys Street door of the Los Angeles Catholic Worker Community's Hospitality Kitchen on Skid Row.

I seemed an unlikely prospect for such a place, such a movement. The heavy silver bracelets that jangled on my wrists as I chopped onions must have seemed as incongruous as my tendency to pontificate about the latest movies while washing lunch trays. (To distinguish me from another volunteer of the same name, I was initially dubbed "Hollywood Larry" by community members.) I thoroughly embarrassed myself by bringing, as my contribution to the first Worker house liturgy/potluck I attended, Gallo wine — at the height of the boycott of that label for its refusal to accept United Farm Worker organization of the migrant workers in its vineyards. (There was a particular irony to this blunder: I never drank the brand myself but had chosen it over the more expensive imports I personally favored in an attempt to exhibit proper Worker "simplicity.")

We did not appear to be a match, the Worker and I. But despite the fact that a deranged man from the soup line threatened me with a butcher knife on my second visit — I recall my biggest concern in that moment was that I would look ridiculous if he actually stabbed me — I kept coming back. Like many people making initial contact with the Catholic Worker, I had little understanding or appreciation of the richness of the movement's vision. What impressed me was voluntary poverty and personal involvement in service to the poor (whom I tended to romanticize along the lines of the noble peasants I'd admired in Italian neo-realist cinema). As for Worker anarchism, I experienced that as the right of certain people to do whatever they liked and the right of the rest of us to put up with it. Arguments for return of the means of production and distribution to workers struck me as anachronistic, since I lacked any understanding of their larger theoretical context in Worker thought. When conversation turned to Catholic Worker farms, I tuned it out — I was passionately enamored of the city.

Clearly not a match. Yet, four or five months later, on the first day of the new year, while having lunch with my oldest friend, I began a conversation about the Worker explaining it "from the outside" and ended up speaking "from the inside" (as best I understood the inside at the time) — an experience, for me, of conversion. Thus began nearly six years of participation in the Los Angeles community.

It was at very nearly the end of those years that I was first asked to prepare a presentation on "Catholic Worker roots." The event was informal — members of the community sat around one evening eating junk food while I spoke for less than an hour from a collection of index cards I'd cobbled together from various sources. At about the same time, Jeff Dietrich — as much of a "leader" as such a self-avowedly anarchistic community would admit to — invited me to write an exposition of Worker philosophy as the preface to a collection of his prison letters which were to be published as *Reluctant Resister*. These two things formed the basis of an evolving series of lectures I have been invited back to present over the following thirteen years, and this present work is the substance of those presentations in written form.

What I have aimed for both in my lectures and in this book is neither academic analysis nor a history of the Worker movement *per se*. Rather, my interest has been a *theological* exploration of the Catholic Worker vision in all its rich and resonating breadth. The goal has been to present and — if I'm to be honest — promote that vision as what I am convinced the movement's founders, Peter Maurin and Dorothy Day, understood it to be: not, finally, a matter of political theory or philosophy (if those things are understood to be subjects for pursuit apart from Christian faith), but rather of profound religious conviction and insight.

Those seeking an academic treatment of the Catholic Worker or its thought would do well to read Mel Piehl's brilliant *Breaking Bread: The Catholic Worker & The Origin of Catholic Radicalism in America*. While I disagree with certain of his conclusions, particularly as to the extent of Peter Maurin's contribution to the "Worker idea," Piehl has set an exceedingly high standard for analysis of the sources and continuing wider impact of the Worker movement and his book has the added advantage of being consistently readable.

As for history, for present purposes it is enough to know only the broadest outlines of the Worker story. There was Dorothy Day — child of bourgeois gentility, active member of the Greenwich Village-Provincetown radical circle of the late teens (which included Emma Goldman, Eugene O'Neill, Max Eastman, Louise Bryant and John Reed), atheist radical journalist for *The Masses*, single mother and then, at the end of 1927, Catholic convert. There was Peter Maurin — French peasant philosopher, former teacher with the Christian Brothers, nonstop talker, essayist and transient. In 1933 they joined forces to publish the first *Catholic Worker* newspaper and distribute it among leftist workers at a May Day rally in New York's Union Square. Actually, Maurin missed the public debut of their creation — he'd had a temporary falling out with Day over the contents of the initial edition.

Day had spent the first thirty years of her life in an internal battle between an intense drawing to Christian faith (specifically, Roman Catholicism) and an equally strong, deeply personal identification with the sufferings of the poor and the struggles of working men and women under capitalism. Until she met Maurin, she saw no way to bring these two things together. Her communist and radical friends had a passion for justice but no transcendent faith, no acknowledged relationship to God. The Church professed to hold the keys of the Kingdom, but most often seemed as oblivious to the inequity and poverty around it as it was to its own enculturation. Then, after an agonized prayer for guidance at the unfinished Shrine of the Immaculate Conception in Washington, D.C. (she was in the city as a journalist covering a hunger march), Day found Peter Maurin at her tenement door. He proceeded to talk for hours, days on end — for four months, in fact. Out of all that talk came a vision for what was to become the Catholic Worker movement, the answer to Day's prayer.

Those seeking more historical information than this might wish to start with Jim Forest's workmanly biography of Dorothy Day, *Love is the Measure*, or with Day's own (self-expurgated) account of her life up through and beyond the beginnings of the movement, *The Long Loneliness* — both of which are still in print. Also available is Robert Ellsberg's excellent anthology of the writings of Dorothy Day, originally titled *By Little and By Little* and now re-issued simply as *Selected Writings*. No longer in print but worth searching out for the wealth of information they contain, despite their stylistic limitations, are three works by William Miller: *A Harsh and Dreadful Love*, a history of the Worker movement up to the time of the book's publication in the early 1970s; *Dorothy Day*, a biography which includes the information Day censored from her own writings; and *All is Grace*, a survey of Day's previously unpublished spiritual journals.

Peter Maurin: Prophet in the 20th Century, by former Catholic Worker Marc Ellis, presents what little biographical information there is about Peter Maurin in the context of the author's own reflections on Maurin's thought — although this book, too, is currently not in print. A determined investigation of a Catholic university library may unearth a copy of Arthur Sheehan's long out-of-print *Peter Maurin: Gay Believer*. Published in 1959, this now misleadingly titled biography benefits from Sheehan's intimate acquaintance with the subject (Dorothy Day, in her introduction to the book, notes that Maurin viewed Sheehan as a "son"), but is handicapped by a style that can only be described as hagiographic.

As depicted by Sheehan, even the most contentious events are recast to give further testimony to Maurin's unfailing wisdom and sanctity. While Dorothy Day wrote on several occasions that she wasn't sure she even *liked* Maurin initially and that he sometimes drove her to distraction with his incessant indoctrination, Sheehan asserts that Day from the beginning delighted in listening to the Frenchman's marathon monologues. Similarly, Maurin's abandonment of Day at the pivotal moment of *The Catholic Worker*'s inception is passed off as an example of his self-effacing pedagogical technique: instruction completed, it was his way to move on, taking his message to new listeners. Despite such spiritualizing evasions, Sheehan's book is in the end a moving tribute, giving one a considerably deeper appreciation for Maurin than is to be obtained from a number of the other works mentioned, which tend to treat him as something of a supporting character within Dorothy's more dramatic story.

It goes without saying that this present work would not exist were it not for the Los Angeles Catholic Worker Community. Of that community I thank in particular Jeff Dietrich and Catherine Morris, who have over the years continued to insist, gently but persistently, that someone not presently choosing to live as a Catholic Worker might still have something of value to say to and for those who have embraced that extraordinary life.

I thank as well my dear friend and companion on the spiritual journey, Katherine Sturtevant, for her always insightful editorial suggestions on the manuscript as it was in process. And finally, I thank my partner Ken Solus, who accepted the burden of reordering our life together to carve out the time and psychic "space" required so that I might face the blank computer screen and begin to write.

Chapter One

An Audacious Vision of Love

In the moving passage with which she closed *The Long Loneliness*, Dorothy Day wrote: "The most significant thing about The Catholic Worker is poverty, some say. The most significant thing is community, others say. We are not alone any more." Forty-three years after these words were published, one could add other voices as well. The conservative Catholic will argue that the essence of the Worker is feeding the poor (movement history is rife with stories of donations made with the proviso "for beans, not propaganda"). The secular progressive may tolerate Worker peculiarities about land and craft, or its focus on liturgical life, because what "really matters" about the movement is its commitment to social justice. Still others seem to discover the core meaning of the Worker in the satisfying fractiousness of such anarchist slogans as "Question Authority" (a maxim which is often to be found blazoned from the battered bumper of a Worker vehicle).

Playing off the existential alienation to which her poignant title alludes, Dorothy Day found the heart of the Worker's meaning in the creation of authentic community: "But the final word is love. ... We have all known the long loneliness and we have learned that the only solution is love and that love comes with community."

It would certainly seem rash to challenge the movement's co-founder regarding the ultimate significance of what she created from the substance of her own life, commitment and passion. Nevertheless, it might well be argued that to focus the meaning of the Catholic Worker too narrowly, even on something as fundamental as "community," risks short-changing the breathtaking ambition of its vision.

Indeed, what is most striking about the now more than sixty years of Catholic Worker reflection, writing and living is the movement's audacity of conviction and action: the unflinching consistency of its call to discipleship; the comprehensiveness of its attempt to bring together all aspects of life into a divinely-ordered, balanced whole; the diversity of philosophical and theological sources it seeks to meld into a unified model for truly human living; the unembarrassed simplicity of its hope.

Various individuals and constituencies may "read" the meaning of the Catholic Worker differently, to be sure. The Communists of the 1930s excoriated it as "clerical fascism" decked out in class-war trimmings designed to fool the proletariat; the anti-war movement of the 1960s celebrated — and diminished — it as simply the "Catholic left." But the Worker remains resolutely beyond the reach of such easy labeling. In some of its beliefs, it stands clearly with the left; in others, it resembles nothing so much as classic libertarianism, that "right wing of the right." This apparent incongruity is due to the fact that, as Dorothy Day and Peter Maurin clearly understood, the Worker vision is so *radical* that it leaves the standard categories of both left and right far behind. Its radicalism (which means "going back to the root," as Peter Maurin liked to remind his listeners) is ultimately grounded not in transitory political or economic theories (though it may borrow from both to articulate and give form to its principles) but in things much deeper, things as old as the divine purpose in creation and as new as the remade heaven and earth of the Eternal Reign of God.

Worker thought takes history seriously, since history is the locus and means of working out that divine purpose, but at the same time it is fundamentally ahistorical, since it makes its judgments and choices from sources outside history as we know it — from God's intent before the fall and God's promise after the consummation of all things in the Commonwealth of Heaven.

A Fundamental Question

In a very real sense, the whole of Catholic Worker theory and practice comes down to a single question: How does one live a consistent, fully human life?

It takes little imagination to realize that simply to ask this question puts one at profound odds with the dominant social forms of our time.

It makes one, to borrow John Paul II's fertile phrase, a "sign of contradiction." And anyone who takes the question seriously enough to base life choices upon the answers obtained is unavoidably an outsider, a troublemaker, a prophet, an agitator, whether he or she seeks that role or not.

This is because there is at work in the world, perhaps now more than at any time before our own, a concerted conspiracy against asking such a question, much less living by its answers. How else can we explain the pervasive effectiveness of dehumanization around us? How else do we account for the desensitizing immediacy of our inescapable culture, a culture that constantly, aggressively and with great psychological and technological skill celebrates and promotes the base, the temporary, the impermanent, the false, the sordid, the violent, the shoddy and that which can be consumed and discarded? How else but as a distraction from the hard work involved in asking and wrestling with the answer to the question of what constitutes authentic human existence?

Assumptions

In beginning to formulate its answer to that question, the Worker does not start with anything new or "original." The assumptions about the nature of reality in which its response is grounded are not things created by Dorothy Day or Peter Maurin; they are all to be found in Hebrew and Christian Scripture, in the teaching of the Church, and in nearly two thousand years of Christian faith and practice.

If there is something distinctive about the manner in which the Worker has dealt with these assumptions (and obviously there is, since Catholic Workers live quite differently than do most Christians), it has to do with shifting the assumptions from the realm of the theoretical, the theological, and the ideal into the arena of immediate daily choice. Indeed, what is singular about the Worker's response to these assumptions is that it dares to believe that they can be enfleshed in the way we live our lives together, do our work, and structure our society. As Peter Maurin wrote in one of his often-repeated "Easy Essays":

What is logical
is practical

even if it is not practiced. ...
The Sermon on the Mount
will be called practical
when Christians make up their mind
to practice it.

That the men and women of the Catholic Worker have, in a unique way, "made up their minds" to attempt to put into concrete practice truths that Christians down through the centuries have affirmed in the abstract goes a long way toward explaining the character and charism of the movement.

The assumptions on which the Catholic Worker vision is premised are rarely articulated directly in the writings of Dorothy Day and others, at least not systematically. Rather, like leaven in dough or the trace scent of incense in a venerable sanctuary, they permeate and are present in all the positions taken, the difficult choices made, the responses to particular issues as they arise. Or perhaps better: like an unseen foundation buried deep in the ground, these assumptions support and give stability to the unfolding, living "building" (in St. Paul's organic sense of the word) that is the Catholic Worker movement — a voluntary association without rules, vows, written constitutions or endowments that has nevertheless not only survived but continued to grow and spread despite the deaths of its founders, nearly unimaginable changes in the world around it, and convictions that place it at dramatic odds with the society in which it now exists and to which it bears witness of a radically alternative way of living.

Even though most Worker writing and action may not directly address them, these assumptions are the place to begin. Unless we understand the movement's premises, much of what the Worker proposes and attempts to live out may seem curious, inconsistent, irrelevant, even quaint. If that is our reaction, we may be tempted to fall back on the comforting notion that what the movement is "really" about is whatever part of its vision fits most snugly into the pre-existing attitudes and convictions that brought us to it in the first place, be they the politics of the left, the works of mercy of traditional Christian piety, or some private disquiet with things as they are.

Such reductionism, however, strips the Catholic Worker of much of its distinctiveness and power. It tames it, makes it manageable on the basis of the far different assumptions of the world in which we must live out our daily lives. But if we confront the Worker vision honestly, in all its fullness, it can only be — depending on our re-sponse — an affront, an unsettling challenge, or a deeply engaging source of hope.

The First Assumption

The first assumption has been made so numbingly trite through pious overuse that it may take us some time and reflection to realize just how profound its meaning and consequences are. That first as-sumption is: **God is love.** Ultimate reality, the source of everything that exists, is — in the deepest and most intimate sense — love. And unlike so much of our love, that love is not sentiment, cheap feeling, the need to control, or a hunger to be useful, appreciated, or affirmed. It is not love that grows from need at all, but rather love that over-flows from fullness. Nor is it what so often substitutes for love in our culture: a kind of disinterested disengagement passing as tolerance — what C.S. Lewis trenchantly terms a "senile benevolence" that ac-cepts anything and everything "so long as the young people are hav-ing a good time."

Rather, the love that is God is a passionate, active, purposeful self-emptying for the highest good of the other, an other to whom ul-timate value is given.

If we take this seriously for a moment, it is nothing short of shocking. It means that God, the ground of reality, is most profoundly God's Self in pouring out that Self for what is *not* God, for the cre-ated. It means that this self-emptying, this on-rush of self-immolation, is the very core of the mystery we approach in coming into the pres-ence of God.

We should note, as well, that to say that "God *is* love" is to say much more than "God is loving." It is to affirm that self-emptying love is ontologically the very "stuff" of divinity. Self-emptying love is God being God. And God being God is a ceaseless activity in which the One with all the power chooses to relinquish that power for the good of the beloved other. God being God is a love that is enfleshed and enacted perfectly in the self-emptying that wedded the uncreated Word with human flesh in the person of Jesus and sent Jesus on the hard road from Nazareth to the cross. Such self-emptying love, the Christian proclaims in joy and awe, is the fundamental fact of the universe. It is our source and it will be our destiny, and not ours only but the whole of creation's.

The Second Assumption

Like the first, the second assumption — though we hear it less often — may seem hackneyed until we consider its consequences. It is: **Every human person is, in and of him or her self, the whole, total, and complete focus of the self-emptying love that burns at the heart of God.** To put the matter in the vernacular of the movies: there are no "supporting roles," there are only starring roles.

Of course, it is part of the mystery of God's being that God can focus fully and perfectly on every single human that ever was, is or will be — and do so, at any point in what we know as time, simultaneously. It is not up to us to sort out how God can do this, how, out of the multiplicity of "stories" that are being lived out at any particular moment, God can give absolute, loving attention to each one. What is ours to do is admit what it means: there are no expendable people.

The Third Assumption

The third assumption, like the first, is something we have probably heard so often that its force has gone stale for us. But again, when we let the truth of it engage us, we may rediscover its shattering power. It is: **every person is an image of God.** That is to say, *every* person — the least, the greatest; the most gifted, the most challenged; the most delightful, the most repellent — is made in the likeness and image of the God who is passionate, self-emptying love, with all the terrible dignity that fact entails.

To regain something of the astonishing meaning of this assertion, we need to remember that, in the ancient world, an "image" was more than a mirror reflection or "little picture" (although it was those things as well); it was an icon that to some extent carried, communicated and participated in the power of the thing it represented — which is one of the reasons the prohibition of graven images was so fundamental a part of the Hebrew religious ethos.

Applied to human persons, then, the affirmation that each of us has been created in the divine image does not mean simply that we are called to some sort of pious game of make-believe along the lines of "wouldn't the world be a better place if we all acted *as if* every person we met were God encountering us?" No! It means that, in actual fact, each person that crosses our path is a living icon of the God that made and sustains all that is. Thus, each person is both glorious in his or her essence and potential and, to some extent, tragic or terrifying in the distortion of such potential through the effects of that breach of God's intent for creation which we call sin.

Clearly, to allow this reality to seep into our consciousness immediately turns everything about the way we normally live with each other on its head, smashing the implicit complacency of our lives.

Suddenly, everyone (and thus, everything) has overwhelming importance. Life and all its choices are discovered to be exploding with moral energy. There are no small issues, just as there are no small people. If God is self-emptying love and if each individual is both the object and a living icon of that love, then there is no one for whom anything less than a full realization of these realities is acceptable.

But this is not, of course, the way we usually live. The dominant society, class, gender or caste at any given point and place in human history tends to posit what we might call a "big story" (which, not surprisingly, is always its own story), which is what God is *really* interested in, and then any number of secondary stories about "the others" who are seen either as obstacles to the goals of the big story, or — at best — sidebars to its overwhelming significance.

The putatively "Christian" civilizations of the West have skirted the patently anti-Christian implications of such self-aggrandizing mythologies by several different theoretical devices which uphold the primacy of the "big story" while appearing to deal with the inconvenient fact of all those other, sometimes competing stories.

One such device is to cast the "other" as a specifically demonic force at war with God's intent in history. This was the case with many of the immigrant Christian interpretations of the conflict with Native Americans in the New World. If the other is a "devil," he is clearly not an image of God and we may, thus, treat him as we will, cheerfully confident that in slaughtering him, enslaving him or divesting him of land we are merely clearing the decks for God's higher purposes centering on us and our kind. We can even be said to be "doing God's work."

An only slightly less pernicious strategy is simply to deny the full humanity of the other, without going on to outright demonization. Such an approach can be seen in some of the theological defenses raised for the slavery of Africans prior to the Civil War.

Finally, Christians have often fallen back on an argument that, while all human persons have their share in the dignity of the divine image, some have been created in God's wisdom for a secondary, supporting role in the human drama (rather like Orwell's famous dictum in *Animal Farm*, "all pigs are equal, but some pigs are more equal than others"). In the ante-bellum South, those who were willing to admit that black slaves were fully human (and therefore to evangelize them) nonetheless justified their enslavement by such an argument. And, it would seem to many, a similar theory is still the basis asserted for limiting the full scope for ministry of women in the Church.

Yet despite these and other like attempts to soften their force, if we truly believe that these first three assumptions express unvarnished reality, then *every* human life, every human story in all its parts, is a shattering, vivid, eternally significant engagement with ultimate meaning — and one which we devalue at our peril. Further, if we accept these first three assumptions as true, how can we feel anything but moral horror and anguish not only at the limiting, dehumanizing suffering of the poor, which blunts and stunts their full development into all they were created by God to be, but also at the soul death of society's "successes," the rich and powerful, cut off from their own full humanity in different but equally deadly ways by the seduction of privilege and the addicting stupefaction of material excess?

We are all inextricably a part of a process which is killing people spiritually at both "ends" of the social spectrum. The "haves" may be doing better than the "have-nots" in certain short-term ways, but — in terms of ultimate reality — everyone is a victim, and it is this fact which underlay Dorothy Day's often-repeated disgust with what she called "this filthy, rotten system."

The Fourth Assumption

The fourth assumption follows logically upon the first three: because God is passionate, engaged, self-emptying love, and because every woman or man that ever lived, lives or shall live is that love's object and image, **every human being has a call**. Each of us confronts a call from God that is built into the nature of reality and the essence of who we are: to express in and through the uniqueness of our personhood, circumstances and moment in history (what we see as our "crosses" as well as our gifts) the reality of self-emptying love, to inject that love into history in the individual way that is ours alone, to enflesh that love for our singular place and moment. Nobody else can do this for us, because nobody else *is* us.

Once again, we are confronted with the truth that every human life, every human story, is profoundly significant because it is irreplaceable. Which means that, from the perspective of reality, the life of the most forgotten, obscure individual — the street person dying of AIDS, the child cut down in tribal war in Rwanda or Bosnia, that most annoying person we must deal with day in and day out in our work — has as much gravity and importance in terms of God's activity in history as the life of any of the "great men" (and the occasional great women) who populate our history books.

The call is the same to each one of us: to bring to life in the particularity of our existential moment that self-emptying love which is the underlying principle of the universe. When we do this, or make it possible for another to do it, in however small a way, our actions — like rocks dropped into a limitless pool — have reverberations that will ripple to eternity. They are that which will last. They are the atoms of the new creation.

The Fifth Assumption

While unambiguously set forth in the two creation stories in Genesis, the fifth assumption is one that the West has by and large ignored, especially since the advent of mercantile capitalism and the triumph of the Industrial Revolution. It is: **A vital part of our imaging of God the Creator, an essential component of the call that is ours as human beings, is to be co-creators with God, vicars and stewards for God of the lavish generosity of God's creation**.

While such a reality has obvious consequences for our use and treatment of the natural order (and forms the basis of what has come to be called Christian Ecology), for the Catholic Worker another less recognized import of this truth has been primary: Our work, our labor, is not just how we earn our keep; it is (or should be) an essential medium for acting out our destiny and dignity as human beings. Work is a "spiritual" issue.

God gives the abundant gifts of creation for the common good. God gives us the ability and the charge to take that abundance and — by our toil, ingenuity and creativity — make it more than it originally was so that we may share it with each other, again for the common good.

This is, in the true meaning of the word, an "awful" task: Our labor is alarmingly sacred. It is not a commodity. It should be a holy act of conscious cooperation in the continuing work of God in the unfolding of creation.

This participation in divine creativity is not the province of a select few: artists, farmers, crafts-workers. Every person born is summoned to it. As our particular talents and gifts differ, so the specifics of how we each individually play our part in this process of ongoing co-creation will differ. But we are less than fully human if we fail to play that part, and if the "system" somehow blocks the ability of anyone to discover, enact and celebrate his or her particular contribution to that process, then something is fundamentally wrong with the system.

The Sixth Assumption

While the sixth assumption would seem the inescapable consequence of the first five, if any of the assumptions could be said to be "original" to Worker thought, at least in its positive and specific articulation, it would be this last: **The ideal society, the best structure for relationships between people, is one that clearly acknowledges the first five assumptions, seeks to embody their truth in all its systems, and is designed to enable all its members to live them out.** (Or, as Peter Maurin more engagingly and simply put it: "We seek to create a world where it is easier for people to be good.")

Every human society, then, also has a call: to affirm not just in pious rhetoric but in the reality of its laws, modes of distribution, customs and attitudes that God (which is to say ultimate reality, by which all else is measured) is love, that every person is the object of that love, that every person is an image of God, that every person is called to enflesh love and to join with God as a co-creator.

Scripture, especially the prophets, tends to uphold this truth in negative form, through judgment. This is not surprising, since such a societal call, heard with any seriousness, is clearly a devastating critique of not only our own society but ultimately of every society ever created by humankind in history. Some may come closer to the mark than others, at least for a time, but all fall short and, inevitably, all finally seek to mask that failure by the creation of an alternative, pseudo-religious ideology grounded in models of power, self-interest and exploitation rather than love, self-emptying and liberation.

Thus, every human society becomes, in biblical terms, "Babylon" — an illegitimate distortion of God's intent for human life. Inevitably, each will posit for itself ultimate moral preeminence, demanding an allegiance that is by rights God's alone. In doing so, each makes of itself a blasphemous counterfeit of the Kingdom of God.

There is a consequence to the collision of this final assumption with the painful facts of human history: Since every human society not only fails to live up to its divinely ordered purpose but also justifies its failure through self-serving ideology at war with the truth, every human society stands under the judgment of God and must be called to repentance. This means that the prophetic stance (truth spoken and enacted in self-emptying love, not in self-righteousness) is not an occasional occupation of God's people but the permanent reality by which they must live until the inauguration of the Age to Come.

A Life of Radical Discontinuity

The Catholic Worker not only embraces these six assumptions as real, but affirms them as capable of incarnation (albeit always imperfectly) in the manner in which we live our daily lives. The movement has grown in an organic, haphazard, sometimes stumbling, "by little and by little" fashion as one practical model for enfleshing its assumptions, for giving them living form. As such, it is not so much a philosophy as it is a way (as the earliest Christians called themselves the "followers of The Way") toward an authentic, faithful human existence — a way to live now, in the immediacy of this existential moment, the two "ends" of the divine intention in creation and consummation. As all faithful Christian life should be, the Catholic Worker is an attempt to infuse history between the fall and the Kingdom with the "lifestyle" of eternity.

In the new heaven and earth that are to come, such a life will be an action of joyful spontaneity; it will conform "naturally" to reality. In the broken world that we now inhabit, however, and of which we are an entangled part, any attempt to live on the basis of these assumptions puts one at war with the given, with what is perceived to be real (even though faith recognizes it as lie).

To affirm these assumptions creates an inescapable confrontation with "things as they are" (or, more accurately, things as they appear to be); it throws us into radical discontinuity with our society and its values. We cannot, in this present world, simply relax into natural conformity to reality. To seek to live in consistency with reality requires choice, discipline, effort and grace, not in the least because we, too, are broken and have Babylon busily at work in our own hearts and minds.

Because we live in a war-zone between the false reality of Babylon and the truth of the Heavenly City, choosing to embrace the real requires actions of pain and renunciation. It requires, in Jesus' phrase, "taking up our cross," and it is a life-long struggle, as evidenced so powerfully in Dorothy Day's own journals. Yet that ongoing struggle is undertaken in the hope and confidence that in striving to live in a manner true to what is real, we will find a joy and freedom beyond our imagining.

The Nature of Hope

We must be clear, however: The hope is not that, in this world's terms, we will "win," be admired, or change everything by tomorrow, in twenty or fifty years. Rather, the hope is that, when we embrace these assumptions and give ourselves to living them out, we tap into something deeper, richer and more lasting than the apparent truth the world offers, because we have cast our lot not with illusion and lies, however comfortable, but with a reality that will stand when all else is consumed in purging fire.

In affirming these assumptions, we trust, as quixotic as it may seem at times, that behind the brokenness, obnoxiousness, despair, weakness, and pain — as well as the beauty and delight — of every human face is truly an image of God. We trust that every human encounter is a holy place where awaits the never-ending rush of light and love that fuel the cosmos.

We trust that if we strive to live by these assumptions, despite our inevitable failures, we are moving toward living in harmony with the fundamental heartbeat of the universe; we are beginning to live real lives that — touched by grace — are built on those things which will last forever.

The Failure of History

In one of the pithy maxims for which he was famous, Peter Maurin pronounced history a "failure." Maurin was not arguing for existential despair; rather, he was countering the prevailing ideological construct of the West since the Enlightenment, the "doctrine of progress."

That doctrine, stripped of its customary high-minded rhetoric, is basically a corporate version of the positive thinking mantra promoted by one self-improvement guru in the 1920s: "Every day in every way I'm getting better and better." The doctrine of progress asserts that, if not every day, at least as a general trend, humanity is steadily getting better and better, extrapolating from the indisputable fact of technological and scientific advance a commensurate moral and spiritual improvement.

Put somewhat crudely, the doctrine of progress would argue: Because we can now walk on the moon, because we have "conquered" many diseases, because we can send television signals around the globe by satellite, because we can explain the natural causes of many things our forebearers thought to be miraculous or demonic, because (at least for a fortunate few) standards of living have risen dramatically, because of all this and much more, people today are in general wiser, more "evolved," and of greater spiritual insight than previous generations. The spiritual and moral tenets of those who came before us are intrinsically suspect, while our own ethical and religious assumptions are automatically more reliable and "scientific." Our ancestors' beliefs were the product of the limitations of their time and place; our convictions are self-evident to a more informed age.

Since this doctrine got its start in the heady era of global exploration, Reformation, Renaissance, and Age of Reason, it is at least somewhat understandable given the very real gains in human knowledge and skill of the time. Similarly, progressive achievements such as the elimination of slavery and the emancipation of women could provide some basis for the endurance of such a sunny notion into the early years of this century. What is less comprehensible is the sur-

.s sort of hubris in the face of Buchenwald and Auschwitz, , and Nagasaki, Baba Yar and the Gulag, My Lai and Saraj. along with countless other monuments to continuing human depravity that have marked the latter two-thirds of this century. To be fair, some commentators would cite a collapse of confidence in the doctrine of progress as one of the primary marks of the post-modern age. But in terms of mass culture, the doctrine's smug ascendancy remains to all intents and purposes intact, if somewhat besmirched by the social graffiti of failed schools, declining standards of living, and a corrosive vulgarization of everyday life.

For Peter Maurin and Dorothy Day, and for the Worker after them, the doctrine of progress is simply a bald-faced lie. Technological advances may be good or bad, depending on how they are put to use, but they have nothing at all to do with moral or spiritual progress. In fact, the Worker tradition would go even further: Not only has technological progress failed to bring any notable improvement in the human soul, but quite the opposite is true. What our culture calls "progress" is, in its moral and spiritual dimensions, not progress at all but a regressive dehumanization that has resulted in an increasing denigration of the dignity of the human person and a systematic abuse and fouling of the good gifts of creation.

In our self-important and remarkably complacent view of our place in history, the unspoken assumption is that our culture represents an apex of human evolution from which we may authoritatively judge all that has preceded us. In such an attitude, Maurin insisted, we are profoundly mistaken. As he wrote in an early issue of *The Catholic Worker*: "There is no such thing as historical progress; the present is in no wise an improvement on the past. . . . The will to power, to well being, to wealth, triumphs over the will to holiness, to genius." Consequently, what most singularly marks our age is the "victory of the bourgeois spirit," which spirit Dorothy Day's biographer William Miller convincingly defines as one of "acquisitive individualism."

In short, from a moral and spiritual perspective (in other words, from the perspective of reality), for all our vaunted "progress," we have lost much more than we've gained.

Secularization

For Maurin (as for the current Pope), the core source of this loss is *secularization* — the idea that social and personal values, moral judgments, and public and private choices as to how we live can be divorced from any grounding in spiritual reality. We presume such matters are infinitely malleable constructs of human will rather than reflections of divine intent built into the very nature of creation. But, as Maurin saw clearly, this splitting of the cultural and political from the spiritual leaves both societies and individuals without any roots, disconnected from the very things that make them what they are created and called to be. For Maurin, secularization was "the great modern error." As he wrote in another of his "Easy Essays":

> When religion
> has nothing to do
> with education,
> education is only information:
> plenty of facts
> but no understanding.
> When religion
> has nothing to do
> with politics,
> politics is only
> factionalism:
> let's turn the rascals out
> so our good friends
> can get in.
> When religion
> has nothing to do
> with business,
> business is only
> commercialism:
> let's get all we can
> while the getting is good.

With secularization, lacking any foundation in relationship to God, God's intent in creation, or our own true nature as images of God, our values become nothing more than current popular opinion. Our fundamental brokenness is never acknowledged and our attempts at moral analysis or discernment flounder in a relativistic sea in which, ultimately, no judgment is permitted. Inevitably, the culture sinks to its lowest common denominator of banality (the sensationalized prurience of the television talk show) or diabolism (the unapologetic celebration of greed and denial of social responsibility of the mid-'90s Republican "revolution").

We think that we can make the system work apart from reality, that we can construct an alternative reality more to our own liking, but the result is only disintegration and chaos: the death of empathy, increasing alienation, addiction on a mass scale, the glamorization of power and violence. Indeed, the system in which we live and whose children we are could not more effectively destroy the human person if it were specifically designed to do so (and, the first Christians would tell us, so it was — by the Father of Lies).

In the face of such all-pervasive catastrophe, is there any alternative to simply succumbing to the culture and its values? There is, Maurin, Day and the Worker would say: reject secularism! Make the difficult but liberating choice to embody reality in our own lives — and do it now, without waiting for anything around us to change.

Metanoia — Begin by Turning

To be sure, such a choice will inevitably start with repentance (the New Testament's "*metanoia*"), because — confronted with reality — we must recognize in grief and humility that we are all part of a massive, insidious revolt against truth. This great rebellion, despite the religious language or symbols with which it may festoon itself from time to time, gives the lie on a practical level to every one of the assumptions we have named. Therefore, it is at war with God and fundamentally corrosive to authentic human existence. Until we are able to admit that this is true, we cannot be effective agents of reality. Until we name our disease, we cannot be healed or become sources of healing for others.

In biblical usage, however, *metanoia* is not just a sorrowful recognition of brokenness. It is a deliberate, conscious turning from that brokenness toward wholeness, an about-face from death to life, from darkness to light. In a very real sense, all the particulars of Worker life, thought and action can be seen as movements of such *metanoia*, conscious choices to turn in a new direction (the direction of reality), and so to confront the lies of Babylon not only by denunciation but also by the simple living out — on one's own responsibility and at personal cost — of the truth of the New Jerusalem.

Sources

Peter Maurin

Peter Maurin, on whose teaching Dorothy Day always insisted all Worker thought was based, was something of a mental pack-rat. Omnivorous in his reading and study, he practiced what he later preached to the Worker: the "cross-pollination of ideas," by which he meant a willingness to integrate into one's thinking anything that resonated with the truth, wherever it was to be found. Not surprisingly, this attitude led him to a creatively selective approach to his sources: He took what he liked and cheerfully ignored those elements which didn't fit his larger vision. It also resulted, upon occasion, in oversimplification or even outright misunderstanding. (In an especially egregious example of the latter, he held up the Catholic missions in California as examples of the sort of voluntary rural communes he was advocating — "the Spanish Franciscans ... succeeded in making willing workers out of the Indians" — when in fact, as is now admitted even by the Church itself, the majority of Native Americans at the missions were kept as forced labor under threat of Spanish arms.)

Despite such occasional lapses, however, Maurin's integrative powers were remarkable. He was not, as Dorothy Day herself admitted, an "original thinker." Rather, his genius lay in synthesis, in discovering connections between his unflinchingly traditionalist Roman Catholicism and a mind-boggling array of political, philosophical and aesthetic theories.

The primary form through which Maurin communicated his message was the deceptively simple "Easy Essay," several of which have already been quoted. Maurin himself appears to have initially referred to these works as "poems" (it was Dorothy's younger brother John who gave them the name by which they are now known), and they certainly utilize a number of poetic devices: repetition, rhythm, and sometimes quite delightful plays on words — as when Maurin notes in one of them that what the world needs is fewer "go-getters" and more "go-givers."

Depending to some extent on one's taste, these "Easy Essays" can seem profound in their simplicity or perplexing in their *faux naif* employment of sing-song cadence, sloganizing and puns. Arthur Sheehan, Maurin's first biographer, stressed that, to understand them properly, one must recognize that the "Essays" were originally intended to be recited aloud, not read on the printed page. It is surely also important to realize that the folksy voice Maurin adopted in these works was a conscious choice, based on his stated conviction that, in order to communicate effectively to working people, profound principles must be expressed in the vernacular of the "man on the street."

Many of the techniques Maurin adopted in his "Essays" may well have had their roots in his training with the Christian Brothers, whose founder, Jean Baptiste de la Salle, enunciated a precise pedagogical theory for the order's educational work among the children of the poor. De la Salle's program stressed, among other things, use of language the student can understand, movement from simple concepts to complex, and constant repetition of a few basic principles — all of which are clearly elements in Maurin's own teaching style in the "Essays."

However they may impress one on first exposure, it is the experience of many that the effectiveness of Maurin's "Essays" grows with repeated consideration. Sometimes they amuse, as when Maurin responded to a critic:

While I don't like some of your ideas,
I like you personally.
I think you are much better
than some of your ideas.

Sometimes they sear the heart with the force of their epigrammatic directness:

We cannot imitate
... Christ by trying to
get all we can.
We can only imitate
... Christ by trying
to give all we can.

And at their best, they can be quietly eloquent, as in the often-reprinted "What the Catholic Worker Believes":

The Catholic Worker believes
in the gentle personalism
of traditional Catholicism.
The Catholic Worker believes
in the personal obligation
of looking after
the needs of our brother.
The Catholic Worker believes
in the daily practice
of the Works of Mercy. ...

The Catholic Worker believes
in creating a new society
in the shell of the old ...
which is not a new philosophy
but a very old philosophy,
a philosophy so old
that it looks like new.

Dorothy Day

It goes without saying that Dorothy Day, steeped in the politics of the turn-of-the-century left and a passionate reader for whom fiction (especially Russian fiction) could speak with near-Scriptural authority, made her own distinctive and significant contributions to Worker thought. A prolific writer, her journalistic style was discursive, personal, non-linear and anecdotal — qualities that led a publisher to reject one of her most cherished projects, a book about Peter Maurin, on the ground that it lacked focus. Despite her somewhat disingenuous claim that all the intellectual content of the movement had its origin with Maurin, Day's own convictions strongly marked the evolving form of what some writers have termed the "Worker idea." In fact, she was not above flatly rejecting Peter's teaching when it conflicted with her own deeply held opinions — as when she, and the Catholic Worker after her, strongly supported various labor actions and boycotts despite Maurin's distaste for conflict and confrontation as strategies of change, a position he summarized in one of his famous epigrams: "Strikes don't strike me."

As much as Maurin was a philosopher, Day was an activist. Considering herself a writer by vocation, she often admitted she could rarely give her writing the time or attention it deserved — there was simply too much to *do*. Sometimes impulsive, always intense, determined, idealistic, she struggled her entire life with a tendency to absolutism, which for her was both a gift and a burden. Part of what made her particular practice of Catholic Christianity so remarkable was that she simply accepted *all* of it and proceeded to live her life accordingly, without the tissue of compromises and accommodations in which so many wrap the severe mercy of the Gospel so as to make it more compatible with life in the world as it is. Capable of scalding wrath ("I hold more temper in one minute than you will in a lifetime," she told one pious critic) and icy withdrawal, she also found the ability to love many, in practical and specific ways, whom most would find particularly unlovable. In the end, it was Day's "luminous spirituality" (as one obituary termed it), more than any other single influence, which formed the character of the Worker movement.

After Maurin's death in 1949, it was certainly Day who took primary responsibility for maintaining — at least in the New York Worker community — a staunchly orthodox Catholic stance in the face of pressure from many both within and without the movement to adopt a less conservative theological position, especially in the tumultuous years following Vatican II. While she was enthusiastic about the post-conciliar Church's renewed emphasis on scripture and its tentative steps toward a more prophetic stance on issues of war and peace, when it came to what some have called the "Protestantization" of Catholic liturgics, theology and mores, Day would have none of it. She was not a fan of priests in T-shirts and gaudy shorts. "It gets so that when I see a priest without his collar staying with us I wonder whether he is on his way out of the Church," reads an entry from her journal in the 1960s. She was troubled by youthful Workers' seemingly casual attitude about making their communions without confession and, sometimes, in a state of "mortal sin." To a nun who wrote to her about leaving her order and joining the Catholic Worker in search of more relevant community, she responded, "with the greatest of sorrow," that every community has its disappointments after the initial rush of newness wears away under the pressures of daily living. Her correspondent would do better to remember her vows, she advised, adding: "the older I get the more I feel that faithfulness and perseverance are the greatest of virtues." When several Workers participated in the publication of a literary magazine with a provocatively obscene title and contents Day found pornographic, she threw them out of the community.

Yet, despite her grief over changes in the Church, the world and the Catholic Worker itself, Day did not despair — of the Church, of the unorthodox, of the movement or of herself either. We must accept a certain sense of failure, she wrote, "in our work, in the work of others around us, since Christ was the world's greatest failure." And seven years after publicly breaking with one young former Worker over issues of the Church's traditional teachings on sexual morality, Day wrote him an unexpected and generous letter, "to apologize for my critical attitudes and to promise to amend my life — or attempt to — by 'mortifying my critical faculties.'"

Day's significance to the Catholic Worker is not just a matter of the impact of her monumental personality. No one has better or more beautifully captured the essence of the movement's spirit and convictions on paper than she. To read her writing, some of it now nearly a half a century old, is to experience anew the paradoxical genius of the "Worker idea," in all its poignant power:

> We were just sitting there talking when Peter Maurin came in.

> We were just sitting there talking when lines of people began to form, saying, "We need bread." We could not say, "Go, be thou filled." If there were six small loaves and a few fishes, we had to divide them. There was always bread.

> We were just sitting there talking and people moved in on us. Let those who can take it, take it. Some moved out and that made room for more. And somehow the walls expanded.

> It all happened while we sat there talking, and it is still going on.

Ammon Hennacy

Of the many others who have come to, gone from and — upon occasion — stayed with the Worker movement, one other deserves particular mention: Ammon Hennacy, whose unique (some might say eccentric) approach to what he termed his "One Man Revolution" was a primary force within the Worker for nearly two decades, beginning in the mid-'40s.

Hennacy was by nature a loner, an egotist, and a vigorous enthusiast for himself and his opposition to war, bourgeois complacency and institutional authority of any kind. Having read the Bible nine times while in solitary confinement as a conscientious objector in World War I, Hennacy had a profound spiritual experience which resulted in a decision to live his life thereafter as completely as possible on the basis of the Sermon on the Mount. To that end, he spent years at hard, manual day labor (to avoid payment of war taxes) and stripped himself of the comforts and security of conventional life.

Hennacy's embrace of Gospel principle did not extend to the niceties of conventional piety, however. He railed at hypocritical priests, false religiosity that ignores social justice, bishops in limousines, and guilt-ridden sexual morality (he considered Dorothy Day puritanical on that subject). Nevertheless he became a convert to Catholicism — later admitting he did so primarily out of infatuation with Dorothy — and was for a time a faithful communicant. He eventually renounced the Church, however, leaving the New York Worker with some bitterness in 1961 and moving to Salt Lake City, where he opened his own House of Hospitality named, with heroic chutzpa, after the I.W.W. martyr to Utah's anti-radical judiciary and mining interests, Joe Hill.

Writing of Hennacy in 1956, Dorothy Day spoke warmly of his vitality and love of life, comparing him to John the Baptist in his sense of mission. Nevertheless, she admitted, he could be "hard to take," since it is "irksome to live with someone who is always right." And, she added, "too-hasty judgments of others and [an] inability to see that he himself is ever wrong — these are his most obvious faults." Yet, she insisted, "Ammon wants to be paid attention to, because he has a message, because he is a prophet." And more often than not, she believed, he was "right, irritatingly right."

Given to signing copies of his modestly titled autobiography, *The Book of Ammon*, with "in Christ the Rebel," Hennacy throughout his life looked to the God he spelled "with a small 'g' and two 'os'" ("the good"), a God who, more often than not, seemed to many a reflection of his own self-confidence. Where some saw passionate prophetic vision and romantic fire, others found braggadocio and vulgar self-centeredness, but — for both better and worse — Ammon Hennacy's personality and particular style have marked the Worker so forcefully that he stands immediately after Maurin and Day in having formative influence on spirit of the movement.

In later decades, numerous other Workers have added their voices, insights, interpretations and emphases, with the result that any attempt to authoritatively lay out the major concepts of the Catholic Worker vision must unavoidably be somewhat arbitrary and less than exhaustive. Nonetheless, certain core ideas can be discerned, ideas which — enfleshed in the daily lives of Catholic Worker communities — give practical shape to that *metanoia*-based life of conscious choice to which reality calls us.

Chapter Two

Spiritual Sources

The Mystical Body of Christ

Dorothy Day often identified the doctrine of the Mystical Body of Christ as the basis for everything the Catholic Worker is and does. This somewhat startling claim is based upon the fact that, with numerous mystics and theologians before her, Day saw in the Mystical Body of Christ an expression of an indissoluble, eternal interconnection of human beings with God and with each other.

The source of that interconnectedness is the Incarnation, in which the Eternal Uncreated takes on created human flesh and, in that inexplicable mystery, not only saves women and men individually from the destruction of unbridled ego attempting to be God unto itself (which is the core meaning of sin), but also takes individual human beings up into the loving oneness of the Trinity. As the Orthodox proclaim: "God became human that humans might become God."

By the Incarnation, Christ (and therefore the undivided Trinity) is now potentially or actually present to us in every other human being. With the Incarnation, human persons are not just images of God (their common gift in creation). They are, if they will only let themselves be, literal dwelling places of the One who cast the galaxies into space and gave life to all that is. Therefore, it is not metaphor to declare that what we humans do to each other is, unmistakably, what we do to God. It is fact.

Further, in the Incarnation we are not only brought into a new unity with God, we are brought into radically deeper and more significant relationship with each other. This is because, as individuals become part of Christ, they also become part of all those countless women and men — past, present and future — who similarly share the divine indwelling. All are together now members not only of a common physical race, a common species, but of a new organism — the Mystical Body of Christ. That organism has as its unifying principle the Holy Spirit, who, as St. Augustine explained, is in Living Being that fire of love which is the fundamental communication perpetually dancing between God Creator and God Redeemer in the Trinity.

If all this is true, if the doctrine of the Mystical Body of Christ expresses reality, then there are immediate, inescapable consequences: No longer is it merely a matter of law that we should care for the weak, minister to the poor, protect the exploited. Rather, as St. Paul points out, it is — in the highest and simplest sense — a matter of what we might call enlightened self-interest that we do so. This is because if any part of the Body suffers, we all suffer. Whether we see it or not, every time human life is diminished, every time a woman or man agonizes needlessly, every time hope is extinguished, every time injustice prevails, we are each in a fundamental and profound way wounded.

In that context, the "radical" social teachings of Jesus (renunciation of worldly goods for the sake of others, turning the other cheek, giving the coat off one's back to another in need) cease to seem idealistic or visionary. They become immensely and immediately practical. What other response could one have to a part of one's own body, to the presence of Christ?

Similarly, the traditional "corporal works of mercy" so emphasized by Maurin and the Worker from its inception (feeding the hungry, healing the sick, clothing the naked, offering hospitality to the homeless, visiting those in prison, burying the dead) cease to be what they always risk becoming in conventional "charity"— a condescending legalism in which one doles out a tithe to the "unfortunate" (with one eye on a promised heavenly reward). Rather, those works are a necessary response to family, to the Head of the family Himself, the incarnate Christ meeting us — as Mother Teresa has often put it — "in His most distressing disguise."

Community

In the truth of the Mystical Body the Worker movement also discerns a consequent fact: We are meant for community, community understood as a place where love is found and given in all the interactions (including the frictions) of daily living and shared fortune.

If we are inescapably and eternally connected in the Mystical Body of Christ, then the practical circumstances of our lives should reflect and embody that connection. If the Mystical Body of Christ is a reality, then we can only escape our calling to community by turning away from an essential element of our humanity.

As twentieth-century Westerners, we often cherish a fantasy of our independence and separateness. In our own culture, this illusion is fostered not only by the much-touted "rugged individualism" of pioneer myth and a romanticized Emersonian "self-reliance," but also, especially in the decades since the Second World War, by an ever-increasing mobility and the anonymity of city and suburb alike. A progressive hacking away of the various limbs of extended family connection and responsibility have reduced our circle of significant relationship to the narrow parameters of a "nuclear family" which is now itself being shattered into the further isolation of single parenting and latchkey children raising themselves.

In the face of such fragmentation, the doctrine of the Mystical Body reminds us that we are united now and forever, whether we choose to recognize it or not. Everything that will last is what holds us together; what will disappear is what appears to separate us. It was Dorothy Day's profound appreciation of this fact (as well as, to be sure, her deep psychological hunger for connectedness — "we are not alone any more") that led her to find the ultimate meaning of the Catholic Worker movement in its creation of community.

Practical Forms

In his teaching on community, Peter Maurin was less interested in logistics than he was in over-arching concept: Whatever specific form Christian community might take, what mattered was *intent* and *inclusiveness*. The intent was to be a conscious choice to enflesh the Kingdom of God. Inclusiveness meant that the distinction between those who minister and those who are "ministered to" must be abolished in a new solidarity in which all become family.

Models for community's functional form were many in Maurin's wide-ranging historical analysis: Christian monasticism, primitive Christian communism (in which, according to the Acts of the Apostles, believers "held all things in common"), the commune tradition of European peasantry, and the communalism of the reformation Anabaptists.

While Maurin articulated the principle, it was left to Dorothy Day and others to make the difficult daily choices that gave substance and reality to his vision. (Indeed, for most of his life with the movement, Maurin lived within the Worker Community very much as did the "guests" from the streets — without his own room, with no regular schedule of work, spending much of his time in conversation and teaching.)

As to the forms arrived at, the first Worker community in New York in the mid-1930s was housed in a cluster of rented apartments centered around Dorothy Day's own Lower East Side tenement flat. In following decades, the community bought several different buildings to provide hospitality for the homeless as well as residences and offices for the Workers themselves. Various Catholic Worker farms were also purchased over the years.

Later Worker communities have chosen a number of differing organizational models (a single, communal "house" being perhaps the most typical), but whatever the specifics, the common threads have been some level of shared resources and commitment to a common work.

As for requirements for "membership" — a term Maurin would no doubt have found odious — unlike its monastic precedents, the Worker has never asked for vows or life commitment, though some communities have required short-term, renewable commitments for full participation in decision-making. In the early days in New York, anyone who showed up and took part in the work was included in the community. Since that time, certain communities have included individuals who work in "outside" jobs and then contribute all or part of their earnings to common funds, while others have required "full-time" commitment to the life and work of the community. Some count as community members only those who actually live in a Worker house or houses, others include individuals who at least to some extent maintain their own residences outside the community.

Whatever the particular form arrived at in any given Worker house, it is important to recognize the inherent tension built into Maurin's two emphases regarding Christian community — that it should be at once *intentional*, based on a conscious choice for the Eternal Reign of God, and *inclusive*, with no distinction between those who join the Worker from conviction and those who find their way to it out of need.

This tension lies in the fact that intentionality, by definition, presumes options. The idealistic young Catholic intellectuals who came to the Worker out of working class or bourgeois backgrounds in the first decades of the movement were making a very conscious and informed choice. Similarly, the members of the counter-culture who gravitated to the Worker in the late 1960s and 1970s (the Los Angeles community was known for years as the "hippie kitchen") were generally the disaffected children of the middle class and they, too, were exercising the luxury of a "downward mobility" available only to those who start from a position of at least some security and affluence.

For the poor, on the other hand, a fundamental element of their poverty is the lack or limitation of options. Downward mobility is not a possibility for those already at the bottom, and an embrace of simplicity or "voluntary poverty" is meaningless for someone to whom such a condition is already an inescapable given.

Thus, the poor — who, in Maurin's vision, are an essential element of authentic community and are to be treated not only as equals, but also as family members — start out from a profoundly different place and often with significantly differing capacities than do those who come to the Worker through conviction and choice. And it is surely here, in the difficult, often wrenching, friction between the tectonic plates of intentionality and inclusiveness, that much of the struggle for faithfulness every Worker community must face on a daily basis is to be found.

It is worth noting that Maurin's model of inclusiveness was to some extent premised on the unique situation of the Great Depression, in which large numbers of the homeless poor were displaced members of the educated middle and skilled working classes. Yet his wide-reaching embrace of the poor as "ambassadors of the gods" (terminology he attributed to the ancient Greeks) certainly took in the more fragile and dysfunctional members at the bottom of the social structure as well, and Catholic Worker history is rich with stories — moving, horrifying, sometimes comical — of attempts to integrate into community the severely wounded.

Personalism

Notwithstanding Dorothy Day's insistence on the primacy of the doctrine of the Mystical Body to Catholic Worker thought and practice, it is Christian personalism that is most often perceived as the defining element of the movement's vision.

Articulated in France before and after the Second World War in the writings of Jacques Maritain and his protégé Emmanuel Mounier, personalism can be seen as an attempt to reassert the traditional Christian doctrine of the dignity of the human person in the face of the dehumanizing processes of mass society in the twentieth century. Confronting social and political realities which conspire to make most individuals feel little more than victims of history's bruising indifference, if not its malevolence, personalism dares assert that every human life has significance beyond itself and that every person can meaningfully participate in and have an effect upon history.

In *The Personalist Manifesto* and his periodical *L'Esprit*, Mounier offered equally stinging critiques of bourgeois capitalism, Marxism and intellectually fashionable existentialism. Moreover, he proposed as an alternative a "philosophy of action" premised on the fundamental primacy of the individual person as a free spiritual and moral agent (hence, "personalism").

While Maurin on numerous occasions referred to Mounier's work as setting forth the underlying principles of his own "program," it should be noted that the concept of personalism is not without historical ambiguity: Enthusiasts for the Worker might be surprised to discover that, in Vichy France, the language of Christian personalism was harnessed to provide theological justification for collaboration with the Nazis and their puppet regime. Less perniciously, in the late 1980s and early 1990s, personalism figured conspicuously in certain Vatican writings of an *Opus Dei* cast. Under the banner of "integralism," these documents revived the "integral Catholicism" concept popular in certain Catholic intellectual circles in the 1920s and 1930s: the idea that although the Church is "above" politics, art and culture, nevertheless, if it plays its divinely appointed role, it will affect all these things through the active efforts of Catholic laity in their respective fields and so become the "glue" uniting a Christian civilization. As utilized by more recent integralist proponents, personalism has provided a philosophical rationale for the view that the laity's primary task is putting into action in the secular world an agenda created, defined and controlled by the hierarchy.

On this latter point, honesty requires admitting that Peter Maurin said exactly the same thing in several of his "Easy Essays," and in terms that might seem bold even to John Paul II. "The appointed leaders of mankind are the Catholic Bishops," he declared in "A Second Open Letter to Father Lord, S.J." In "When Christ is King," he was equally unequivocal:

When Christ is the Leader
the priest is the mediator.
When Christ is the Leader
the educator
trains the minds of the pupils
so that they may understand
the message of the priest.
When Christ is the Leader
the politician
assures law and order
according to the priest's teachings.

Yet Christian personalism as finally understood by the Worker is neither a call to passive acceptance of evils one is presumably powerless to change nor a theological argument for the laity knowing (and keeping to) its place. Rather, as proclaimed and lived in the Worker, personalism affirms that every human being, as an image of God and a recipient of divine love, is a significant "player" in the meaning of history; each individual is a subject "actor" in the immediacy of his or her situation, not just an object of history.

Further, since the ultimate meaning of human history is redemptive (God making all things into the Kingdom, in which *zedakah*, "rightness," is made perfect), each of us is called and has opportunity and responsibility to participate actively in history as a knowing, willing medium of that redemption.

In personalism, there is an essential connection between our individual redemption and the redemption of the entire universe. We are not just "saved" from damnation and promised an eternity with God. We are offered a sublime, terrifying mission: to take our small piece of the human story and infuse it with the self-emptying love which is the means both of our personal salvation and of the regeneration of the cosmos.

How are we to do this? By making deliberate, conscious choices in the dailiness of our lives to inject divine love into that portion of history which is ours alone and no one else's. To be sure, the strength, the will, even the desire to do so is a gift of God, and God *is* in fact that very self-emptying love we are called to release into our world, but the choices are ours, and in those choices lies the meaning of our existence.

We may protest that we are so small, so powerless, that we have so few resources. That does not matter, personalism assures us. We can nonetheless make significant decisions — "on our own responsibility," as Peter Maurin liked to say. We need not wait for the world, for institutions, for the church, for the political "situation," for anybody or anything to catch up, change, or make it easier for us. Once we have seen the reality of who God is and what we are created and called to be, once we have been touched by God's Spirit, we must start living by that reality, right now, right here, with what is at hand, believing that wherever need, hunger, loneliness, injustice or woundedness confronts us in the ordinariness of our present life is the very place where now, today, we can begin to choose to participate in God's redemptive work.

Clearly, such conviction gives tremendous consequence to every human life and all its actions. It means that the smallest choice to enflesh divine love is a choice that claims and celebrates our dignity as human beings created in God's image. It means that, by these small decisions and actions (whether they be successful or humiliating failures in terms of result), we become part of an ongoing operation of love which we will see clearly, in the consummation of all things, to have been the point of the whole great redemptive "drama" in the first place.

Personalism affirms that when we actively bring self-emptying love into our particular moment and place in history we are not only made more fully human, we *move* history (the true, lasting history) more vitally than do generals, presidents, power-brokers or persons of "influence." In the personalist decision to become a channel for enacted love, our lives are made the fuel of God's continuing purpose. Therefore, we must act, sometimes foolishly in the world's eyes; we must take risks — like those fishermen in Galilee who were challenged to drop everything and follow *now*.

The personalist does not wring his hands and say "something should be done." The personalist rolls up her sleeves and does something. This is because to believe and practice personalism is to trust that genuine change, redemptive change, much more often surges up than it trickles down; surges up from individual choice, from personal responsibility, and with results that, while not necessarily "successful" in the world's terms, will last into eternity. When all things are made new, these personalist acts will still be there, purged of ego and glorious, because they are the places where reality was allowed to break through and transform history.

Yet despite this hope, Worker personalism is tough. It knows that, in a broken world drunk on lies, there will be inevitable opposition to actions of faithfulness to redemptive truth. Personalism costs. It calls us to an embrace of our limitations; it invites us to stand with the weak, the poor, the anguished and the despised, not just because they need us, but because we recognize that we are already one with them. Personalism challenges us to let go of the safety nets of privilege, the protections and security we so carefully build into our lives.

This is no easy thing — it led Christ to a Roman cross. But, personalism challenges us, it is the *necessary* thing. It is true, as Dorothy Day so often quoted Dostoyevsky, that "Love in reality is a harsh and dreadful thing compared to love in dreams." Yet anything less is a failure to live up to the significance of who we are.

Voluntary Poverty

As Dorothy Day noted in her closing words to *The Long Loneliness*, for many people voluntary poverty is the most significant thing about the Catholic Worker. Wearing castoff clothes, begging for the food they share with their guests, foregoing the panoply of things now considered essential to an adequate standard of living, Catholic Workers have for over sixty years followed Maurin's teaching and example by choosing to live within the same limitations as those they serve, never forgetting that, by virtue of its being a choice, such poverty is profoundly different from that experienced by the poor.

Certainly no element of Worker life has a more venerable history than its embrace of what St. Francis affectionately dubbed "Sister Poverty." The teaching of Jesus in the Gospels still has the power to profoundly disturb the comfortable hearer: "Woe to you who are rich.

... You cannot serve God and money. ... It is easier for a camel to pass through the eye of the needle than for a rich person to enter heaven. ... Do not lay up treasure for yourself on earth where moth and rust corrupt, or thieves break in and steal. ... If you want to be perfect, go and sell all you have and give the money to the poor."

The early Fathers were no less exacting, and Dorothy Day quoted them more than once: "The bread you retain belongs to the hungry, the garment you lock up is the property of the naked;" and "What is superfluous for one's need is to be regarded as plunder if one retains it for one's self."

From the earliest days of the church, however, when Ananias and Sapphira attempted to hold back a portion of their gift to the common apostolic fund (Acts 5), Christians have struggled with the apparent absolutism of their Lord's verdict on money and possessions, and the security we convince ourselves these things can provide.

It did not escape Maurin's notice that it was only with the rise of mercantile capitalism that the traditional Christian judgment on the pursuit and accumulation of wealth was theologically compromised. He also recognized that it was at this same point in history that the Church's previously unwavering condemnation of usury, lending money at interest (a foundational principle of the capitalist system), was reinterpreted as lending money at *excessive* interest and thereby rendered — for all practical purposes — meaningless.

To be sure, there had been rich Christians prior to the Renaissance, some of them "princes" of the church, but until the end of the Middle Ages all Christendom had recognized, at least in theory, that such affluence was spiritually problematic.

It took the Protestant divines of Calvin's Geneva to turn Christ's teaching on its head and proclaim, by a selective appeal to certain Old Testament passages, that wealth is in fact a testimony to God's election, poverty the result of personal sin, and the pursuit of profit a primary responsibility of the godly man. What Jesus condemned was not the pursuit of wealth in itself, these theological innovators insisted, no matter how his unvarnished words might appear to read. No, what he denounced was rather such pursuit by ungodly means, a sensual excess in luxury, an idolatrous attachment to one's riches. The poverty the Lord had commended was also reinterpreted: It was now to be understood as consisting in an inward spiritual disposition having nothing at all to do with the hard facts of economic life. Indeed, the actual poor, far from being the "blessed" of Christ's beatitudes, were suffering the natural consequences of their own sloth, depravity and vice.

To be fair, it must be acknowledged that not all the spiritual descendants of Geneva adopted so bald-faced a rejection of the Christian tradition regarding wealth and poverty. A number of middle-class English evangelical groups in the eighteenth and early nineteenth centuries, for example, combined a Reformed zeal for profit with the conviction that, for a Christian, the pursuit of wealth was to have as its motive doing the most good possible with the money one made. Such "enthusiasts" (as they were dismissively labeled by the establishment) included the well-to-do Clapham Sect among Anglicans, prominent in the fight to abolish the slave trade, and, among nonconformists, the Methodists with their open-air meetings aimed directly at the unchurched urban working class.

Despite their funding of missionary work, Bible societies, education for the underprivileged, and moral and spiritual improvement projects for the poor, however, these undeniably holy and sincerely committed evangelicals nevertheless failed to perceive that much of their wealth was, at least indirectly, built upon the injustices of expanding industrialization and the British colonial system. Accepting the prevailing view that poverty was a result of individual sin, not systemic social evil, they were in general as insensitive to the condescension implicit in their good works as they were to the distance their affluence and respectability created between themselves and the beneficiaries of their charity.

Similarly, when the "Social Gospel" burst upon and divided American Protestantism at the end of the nineteenth century with its proclamation that Christ came not only to save individual souls but to conform human society to the Kingdom of God, it remained for all its moral fervor and idealism a fundamentally bourgeois construct. While a few of its more radical proponents dared to call for a less inequitable distribution of wealth or to critique certain of the secondary structures of entrepreneurial capitalism, by and large the movement accepted the system as it found it, looking to private philanthropy and a kind of benevolent paternalism to "improve" the "defective and dependent classes," as one Social Gospel advocate termed them.

While the Roman Catholic Church was never entirely comfortable with Protestant revisionism regarding money and possessions, it had effected an uneasy accommodation on these matters long before the triumph of capitalism, an accommodation it accomplished by splitting the body of the faithful into two discrete parts. Those called to the "way of perfection" as religious brothers or sisters were to embrace poverty. Garden-variety Christians, on the other hand, were not bound by the dominical counsels so long as they supported the Church financially and practiced charity to the extent their means allowed. It appeared an adroit compromise: by the monk's or nun's vow of poverty, the Church retained a living witness to the traditional Christian teaching on wealth; by its relaxation of that standard for ordinary folk, it made its peace with the world. Maurin, however, for all his respect for the Church's wisdom, would have none of it. "The Counsels of the Gospels are for everybody," he often insisted, not just for religious under vows.

For Maurin, Day and the Worker, however, the poverty which Christ's followers are encouraged to embrace is always distinguished from the absolute destitution of the poorest of the poor. It is true that Maurin himself often lived without a change of clothing or a bed of his own — on more than one occasion he handed on the extra shirt specially provided him to someone else in greater need and inevitably any room set aside for his use ended up being given over to others. Nonetheless, despite his personal manner of life, he always spoke of voluntary poverty in terms of each person having simple sufficiency, with any surplus being understood as God's provision for meeting the needs of others. In addition, for the Worker, poverty meant and means more than a simple lack of financial resources and the things such resources can buy. True, like the mendicant orders, Catholic Workers would accept personal and communal poverty voluntarily and place themselves alongside those they served by accepting the role of beggar, spending their energies ministering to the poor and working for justice and peace rather than earning money. But the Worker was to embrace other, more subtle, aspects of Sister Poverty as well: what Dorothy Day termed the "precarity" with which the poor must always live, the marginalization that comes with exclusion from conventionally acceptable standards of living, and, with these things, the shame of poverty.

"Precarity" is a word Dorothy Day used (and possibly coined) to signify the permanent lack of security and dependence on circumstances outside one's own control which characterize the life of the poor. For her, precarity was valuable not only because it provides a means of experiencing life as the poor must experience it, but also because it serves as a constant reminder of our utter dependence on

God. That dependence, she understood, is an offense to the spirit of this age, in which self-sufficiency and the attendant notion of our entitlement to what we have effectively blind us to the reality that every breath we take, every morsel of food we consume, every skill or talent by which we earn our living — in short *everything* — comes to us from God as a gift. We are responsible, to be sure, for what we do with these gifts, but we must never lose sight of the fact that their origin is not ourselves but the One who is source of every good thing. Sharing the precarity of the poor helps us keep this truth in view.

Such precarity has been made real again and again over the years as various Worker houses have faced lines of hungry men and women with only "five loaves and a few small fish," literally "praying in" the additional money or food necessary to meet the requirements of that day. Further, in demonstration of a positive commitment to precarity, and to the consternation of some of their supporters, Worker communities blessed with donations beyond their immediate needs have over the years disbursed their surplus to less well-supplied communities or other groups working for social change, rather than keep the excess as security against some future need.

The marginalization that is a daily reality for the poor likewise has constructive value when taken on voluntarily. By setting us outside the sanctioned presumptions and mythologies of mainstream culture, such marginalization can free us to see that culture and its self-serving distortions with new clarity. As we view the dominant system through the eyes of its victims and losers, we gain a potentially more accurate critical perspective which, in itself, can provide necessary spiritual detoxification. Standing with the poor in their banishment from the charmed circle of those whose lives are counted important, whose opinions are taken seriously, we can find in our newly discovered helplessness, frustration and even rage the beginnings of a fresh and more Gospel-ready understanding of our world.

Examples abound: from the comfort of a middle class existence, legislation funding tax breaks for the wealthy through reduction of social services for the poor may strike us as unjust in the abstract. That abstraction will take on powerful specificity, however, when those with whom we live out our daily life, those we love as family, are the ones who will bear the all too real brunt of such legislative decisions. Similarly, when we cast our lot with the poor and rely with them on a county hospital for our care, proposals to cut funding for public health will have a new and shattering relevance.

In the marginalization that comes with voluntary poverty, we also begin to experience for ourselves the shame of the poor. It is hardly surprising, in a culture in which the highest values are success, wealth and power, that poverty and its attendant powerlessness should be seen as shameful. That the poor internalize this shame, consciously or not, often deadening its force by self-destructive addictions, would seem self-evident. What may surprise us, however, is the extent to which we recoil from personally sharing in that shame, even when we think we are moving toward freedom from the false judgments and misplaced values of the society around us. It is one thing to act compassionately *for* the poor; it is quite another to be confused *with* them. In this regard, a former Catholic Worker recounts the searing embarrassment he felt at a Social Security office when, navigating a mentally limited homeless woman through the complicated application process for Supplemental Security Income, he was mistaken for her husband. Other Workers have felt the force of such shame in the hostility, depersonalization and sexual objectification they have endured while being imprisoned for acts of conscience and prophetic witness.

It may be, as well, that Peter Maurin's emphasis on the spiritual importance of begging can best be understood within the context of this willing embrace of the shame of poverty. Like precarity, begging reminds us on a daily basis of our dependence on divine providence, to be sure. But it also, again and again, day after day, puts us in the position of the poor: We must ask for what we need, ask knowing we may be rebuffed or ignored, and in asking admit that we are not self-sufficient, that we are "failures" by the standards of this world.

The Catholic Worker insists that the poverty of the poor in reality carries no shame *for them*, though it should shame the society that creates such poverty and allows it to continue. Yet at the same time, perhaps paradoxically, the Worker urges the willing shouldering of just that perceived shame of poverty on the part of those who would stand with the poor and so with Christ. This voluntary acceptance of the psychological as well as the physical consequences of poverty, Dorothy Day understood clearly, is a vital part of the incarnational model of self-emptying love to which the personalist is called.

For the Worker, voluntary poverty is not taken on out of some sort of spiritual masochism (as has been the tendency with some traditional forms of Catholic piety). It is not a penance. Neither is it required because the gifts and pleasures of the material world are evil in and of themselves. Rather, voluntary poverty is welcomed so that we might live with *integrity*, in authentic solidarity with the poor — those we serve, those on whose behalf we speak out against injustice, those we empower to speak out for themselves. Poverty is adopted gladly, because in it we discover liberation. As we let go of the comforts and protections of the bourgeois world, we find ourselves free to make personalist choices without having to calculate their potential cost. We have nothing left to lose. As Dorothy Day wrote:

> Once we begin not to worry about what kind of house we are living in, what kind of clothes we are wearing, we have time ... to remember that we are our brother's keeper, and that we must not only care for his needs as far as we are immediately able, but try to build a better world.

Finally, although Maurin himself never spoke of it, the fact is that our acceptance of voluntary poverty calls the poor themselves to a new honesty in their dealings with us as we live and serve among them, an honesty which is the opposite of the manipulation of guilt on which so many "panhandlers" must rely. If, like St. Peter, we can honestly say to those in need "silver and gold have I none, but what I have I give," if instead of a handout we offer a place with us around our own simple table, a bed under our own roof, then an opportunity is opened for breaking through the inevitable (and justifiable) resentment which must come with the unequal balance of power prevailing when one gives from surfeit and the other asks out of desperate need. When our own manner of living makes clear that the gift comes as justice, not "charity," when who we are is no longer an affront to the daily afflictions of the poor, then the truth of St. Vincent de Paul's piercing observation will find a home in our midst — "It is only for your love alone that the poor will forgive you the bread you give to them."

Chapter Three

Political Sources

Philosophical Anarchism

Perhaps the least appreciated element of Catholic Worker thought over the years has been the movement's stubborn espousal of anarchism. As Dorothy Day once noted in her column, "this is the ... label which confuses many of our readers (especially the bishops?)." The Worker's sometimes erratic attempts to incarnate anarchistic principle in its own practice have often left a good number of its supporters baffled, if not infuriated.

On the most basic level, hesitation regarding the Worker's anarchist stance no doubt reflects the fact that, in the popular mind (formed in large part by media usage), anarchy is understood simply as a complete collapse of social order: that ultimate and horrific state of chaos in which the strongest and most brutal run rampant without restraint, bringing down spoilation, violence and death upon the weak and unprotected in the process. The difficulty of countering this misconception with the true meaning of philosophical anarchism is complicated by the fact that, both in its tenets and action, anarchism is intrinsically resistant to clear-cut, authoritative definition.

Those calling themselves anarchists represent a wide range of apparently contradictory convictions: pacifists and advocates of violent class warfare, atheists and mystics, confrontationalists and conciliatory exemplars. That such diversity can be tolerated within one philosophical viewpoint is due in large measure to the fact that anarchism as a matter of principle rejects compulsory schemes and refuses to lay down any absolute blueprint for the ideal social construct. Rather, it holds up more generalized goals: a society in which all individuals may do whatever they choose, so long as they do not interfere with the freedom of others to do the same; a society in which class distinctions have been eradicated and, with them, those economic and social inequities which inevitably limit free choice; a society in which organizational relationships are deliberately reduced to a human scale (as opposed to the massive, impersonal systems of nation and bureaucracy).

For all anarchists, whatever their differences on other points, the fundamental principle is the absolute primacy of human freedom. From this principle follows naturally an implacable opposition to any institutionalized coercive relationship, whether it be government, the wage system, the landlord system, monopoly capitalism, colonialism, bureaucracy, patriarchy, oligarchy or the dictatorship of the proletariat. Not surprisingly, this opposition finds its primary expression in a profound hostility toward that ultimately coercive institution: the state.

By its very nature, the state begins with the mass rather than the individual, imposing social cohesion and direction from above. In so doing, it must inevitably employ compulsion, actual or implied, to enforce its policies on at least a significant portion of its people. Further, the function of such compulsion remains always and everywhere the same: to protect the power of the few and enforce the compliance — if not the outright exploitation — of the many. This is true, the anarchist argues, whether a particular government be monarchical, republican or totalitarian (of either the socialist or fascist stripe).

Based upon this understanding of the nature and purpose of government, anarchists unabashedly assert their commitment to the abolition of the state, renouncing on principle both its authority over themselves and any legitimizing participation in its processes — organizing parties, supporting candidates, running for office or voting. (It was on precisely this basis that Dorothy Day in her youth refused to join in demands for the enfranchisement of women and, throughout her life, never registered to vote.)

Rejecting the shifting political coalitions and compromises of bourgeois politics ("majority rule ... is always mediocrity rule," wrote Russian anarchist Prince Peter Kropotkin), anarchists propose instead spontaneous, fluid social relationships based on voluntary cooperation for the common good. The sole legitimate purpose of such cooperative efforts is understood to be the satisfaction of the *necessary* requirements of *every* member of the community (as opposed to the superfluous desires of the few). Whatever specific social structures are required must be consciously kept to a minimum, always limited to strictly functional significance and immediately dismantled once their usefulness is at an end. They are never to be institutionalized so as to supplant personal choice, responsibility and initiative. Despite this determination to protect untrammeled freedom, however, the goal of such libertarianism is ultimately not isolative but unitive: Men and women must be free so that, in their freedom, they might act on their own authority to forge the justice of truly egalitarian community.

Clearly, such a paradigm requires an extraordinarily high level of personal responsibility. Indeed, it could be said — to put the matter in psychological terms — that anarchism calls for the growth of every person out of infantilization and dependency, whether willing or imposed, into his or her full stature as a human being. Contrary to the criticism often leveled against it, the anarchistic vision is anything but a defense of egocentric gratification or puerile self-indulgence. To the contrary, it is a challenge to the highest and most demanding model of maturity. For the committed philosophical anarchist, freedom is the most costly, exacting option of all.

Anarcho-Syndicalism

All anarchists believe that workers should determine what work they do, how they work, and with whom they work. Some anarchists, however, take the concept of workers' control still further, making it the basic principle of all social organization. These are the anarcho-syndicalists (from the French "*syndicat*," meaning trade union).

As do all anarchists, anarcho-syndicalists hold that authentic authority lies absolutely in the individual in himself or herself. It cannot come from outside or from above, it can only come from within — anything less reduces and compromises the fullness of human dignity. Yet, if we are to live together and function in harmony for the common good, we must have some serviceable method for balancing the inviolable freedom of the individual with the needs of the community.

The solution anarcho-syndicalism proposes to the conundrum created by the competing values of personal liberty and corporate solidarity is a voluntary collective of workers in which those who hold decision-making power are also those who will be affected by the decisions made. Some anarcho-syndicalists admit the possibility of relatively large-scale workers' collectives (all the employees of a factory, for example), operating through the democratic election of representatives. And certain theorists have gone on to propose an ever-widening pyramid of interrelated workers' committees electing delegates to regional, national and even international "legislatures" of workers. For most, however, the anarcho-syndicalist ideal is best expressed in groupings small enough so that each worker has a voice and each shares in responsibility for the decisions made. In such a collective, no individual is lost in the mass. Instead, each person is empowered, called to personal responsibility, taken seriously. This "cell" of workers, freely joined together, is — for the anarcho-syndicalist — the essential building block of the new order.

In the United States, anarcho-syndicalist ideas had significant influence in the "one big union" of the Industrial Workers of the World (nicknamed "Wobblies") founded in Chicago in 1905 by a diverse group of some two hundred socialists and trade-unionists including Mother Jones, Eugene Debs and "Big" Bill Haywood. With its outreach to female, African-American, unskilled and non-English speaking workers disdained by the skilled craft-workers of the American Federation of Labor, the I.W.W. held continuing appeal for Dorothy Day, who had herself proudly carried a red I.W.W. card as a young journalist in the 'teens. Later, she was to see fruitful parallels between certain anarcho-syndicalist elements of the I.W.W. program and the medieval guild system of which Peter Maurin often spoke approvingly. Maurin himself — despite a profound antipathy to the foundational Wobbly doctrine of class conflict — was ready to borrow I.W.W. concepts when they fit his larger purposes, in particular the union's commitment to abolition of the wage system and, perhaps most memorably, its notion of a "new society growing up in the shell of the old." Given such precedents, it is understandable that, in its anarchism, the Catholic Worker has always partaken deeply of the fiery spirit of the Wobblies and their dynamic vision for a new social order "wherein justice dwelleth."

Anarchist Means for Change

As noted, anarchists reject the political paradigm, which — even when employed by socialists or Marxists — relies upon the power of the state, imposes its program from above and attempts to effect change by obtaining control of the mechanisms of coercion, whether through the ballot box or by violent revolution. Having abandoned the political arena, then, anarchists generally propose four complementary methods for the advancement of their vision for social change, each of which has had its distinct impact upon Worker practice: the power of example, proletarian education, publication and "Direct Action."

Influence by Example

Anarchists believe that deep within each human heart lies a hunger for the authentic human dignity which only true liberty can provide, however perverted, blunted or squelched that hunger may be by social or psychological circumstances. When, therefore, people observe a man or woman acting responsibly in the full authority of his or her ontological freedom, without concern for whatever systematic restraints may exist in society and with willing acceptance of the inevitable price of such an exercise of personal power, this example of independent moral sovereignty challenges, liberates and — at least for a few — inspires change. As a result, simply by living out their convictions, anarchists consider themselves to be serving as active agents for altering the perceptions, and eventually the behavior, of those around them.

A venerable Catholic Worker story gives vivid witness to Peter Maurin's personal commitment to this anarchistic style of influence. When rocks needed to be broken to prepare a road on the Catholic Worker farm, Maurin never suggested direct participation in the work to anyone. Rather, following a general announcement of the project, he each morning thereafter laid out the necessary tools at the site and himself began breaking stones, trusting that others would be drawn by his good efforts. There is unfortunately no record of how many of those then in residence felt led to join Maurin in his labors, but on another occasion a young Catholic Worker observed that — at least with some people — trusting in the power of example was like "throwing peanuts at a tank."

Education

Along with influence by example, education of the proletariat has always figured largely in anarchist theory. In fact, German anarchist Rudolph Rocker once termed the anarcho-syndicalist union a "school for the intellectual training of workers." In such a school, laboring men and women could come to see the meaning and sources of their predicament, the connections between various apparently discrete social problems, and the potential solution to those problems through anarchistic revolution. At the same time, as Rocker noted, the workers' school was to provide not only theory and analysis but also practical training that would ready the worker to take his or her place in (and help shape) the new order once the revolutionary moment arrived.

To that end, turn-of-the-century anarchist "schools" — in many cases focusing particularly on immigrants and most of them decidedly *ad hoc* affairs — included indoctrination in radical theory and history, English language classes, training in practical managerial skills (for the factories that anarcho-syndicalists expected to take over and reorganize), and a wide range of cultural and self-improvement courses.

From its earliest days, the Worker movement reflected this anarchist tradition of proletarian education. As discussed in greater detail in the following chapter, Maurin often affirmed the importance of scholars sharing their knowledge with the workers — and of working people imparting their practical skills to intellectuals, as well. Indeed, one of the first "outreach" programs the fledgling New York community attempted was a storefront office Maurin and a friendly university professor opened in Harlem in 1934. Though it was a decidedly modest undertaking, lacking even electricity, this project offered — along with Maurin's inevitable discourses — storytelling and art classes for African-American children and foreign language lessons for adults (the later provided by the professor). Throughout the 1930s and 1940s, the Worker continued to provide a forum in which specialists in everything from economics to liturgical arts could offer their expertise to working men and women who would otherwise never have had the opportunity for such exposure.

Publication

The most visible arm of anarchist endeavor was, historically, the "propaganda of the word." Although anarchist publication declined drastically after World War I, during the last two decades of the nineteenth century and the first fifteen years of the twentieth, a number of anarchist journals — from ephemeral flyers and broadsheets to established dailies with wide readership — flooded immigrant working class communities. After its founding in 1905, the I.W.W. took such propaganda to new and more sophisticated levels, adding powerful graphics, cartoons and even — in its justly famous *Little Red Songbook* — compilations of revolutionary songs, many of which were the work of I.W.W. martyr Joe Hill, after whom Ammon Hennacy named the House of Hospitality he opened in Salt Lake City in the 1960s.

Peter Maurin's suggestion to Dorothy Day that she start a Catholic radical paper for working people is often interpreted as evidence of his view that one should take whatever skills one has and place them at the service of the common good. Day had experience as a journalist and considered herself by vocation a writer. It was logical for her, therefore, to put that background to work for the personalist revolution. Given the vital history of the anarchist press, however, it would seem likely that its precedent also provided at least an indirect context for the launching of Day's Catholic-personalist publication. Like many an anarchist journal, *The Catholic Worker* began on a shoestring, faced a highly uncertain future (the first issue admitted that "whether it will be a monthly, a fortnightly or a weekly ... depends on the funds collected for the printing and distribution") and reflected the editorial viewpoint of a very small group — just two people, in fact, when it began: Dorothy Day and Peter Maurin. There is more than a little irony to the fact that, as noted in the *Encyclopedia of the American Left*, the "most influential of quasi-anarchist papers" in the United States after the First World War was none other than *The Catholic Worker* itself — even though its "religious (even papal) anarchism" was "ideologically anathema to old-time anarchists."

Direct Action

While example, education and journalism are all important anarchist tools for change, the most distinctive anarchist method has always been and continues to be Direct Action. As the term was originally used among anarchists, in particular anarcho-syndicalists, Direct Action was understood to mean strikes, boycotts, sabotage, and — in extreme instances — armed resistance or insurrection. As it has come to be more generally understood, however, Direct Action refers to any step taken to remedy an evil, correct an injustice, or meet a human need **by the most immediately effective means possible**, without recourse to the more indirect methods of political action — editorializing, petitioning, lobbying, coalition building, and ballot initiative.

Put simply, Direct Action insists: If something is wrong, fix it yourself — again, as Peter Maurin said — "on your own responsibility." If an injustice is being perpetrated, step in and stop it. If the situation is not amenable to individual correction, then protest, draw attention, raise as much hell as you can so that the continuing operation of that injustice will be frustrated to the maximum extent possible.

If one were a Polish villager in 1944, for example, watching cattle cars full of Jews pass through one's town every day on the way to Auschwitz, a commitment to Direct Action would mean one would not just express concern quietly to one's friends, or even take the admittedly heroic step in that historical context of writing a letter of inquiry or protest to local officials or the newspaper. Rather, one might go out and sit on the tracks to block the train, blow up the tracks in the night, or join with others to attack a train and liberate the captive Jews. Alternatively, if the train stopped in the village for some reason, one might speak to the guards and urge them on the basis of conscience to release their captives. These and any number of other possibilities would all be instances of Direct Action. What all of them have in common is a willingness to become personally, directly involved in the matter at issue, rather than remaining protected by the buffering processes of "official channels" or the delegation of accountability through more conventional political means.

Such an admittedly extreme example as this is useful in that it highlights an inevitable corollary of the personal responsibility assumed in Direct Action: personal *risk*. To be sure, not all Direct Action is as dangerous as an attempt to intervene in Nazi genocide. Yet risk of some sort is nearly always involved, and over the years the Catholic Worker has been no stranger to such jeopardy, as when, from the 1970s until 1991, a number of Workers were imprisoned for sitting on tracks leading to the Rocky Flats, Colorado, plant where the plutonium triggers for all U.S. thermonuclear weapons were being produced, thereby — at least temporarily — delaying shipments of radioactive materials.

To Peter Maurin, the Church's venerable works of mercy were the most basic and necessary form of Direct Action available to the Christian. If you see someone hungry, offer a place at your own table. If you see someone homeless, provide shelter under your own roof. If someone comes to you without sufficient clothing, share your own. And do it all on your own responsibility. As Dorothy Day wrote in 1942:

> No one asked us to do this work. The mayor of the city did not come along and ask us to run a bread line or a hospice to supplement the municipal lodging house. Nor did the Bishop or Cardinal ask that we help out the Catholic Charities in their endeavor to help the poor. No one asked us to start an agency or an institution of any kind. On our responsibility, because we are our brother's keeper, because of a sense of personal responsibility, we began to try to see Christ in each one that came to us. If a man came in hungry, there was always something in the ice box. If he needed a bed and we were crowded, there was always a quarter around to buy a bed on the Bowery. If he needed clothes, there were our friends to be appealed to, after we had taken the extra coat out of the closet first, of course.

Ironically, the instinctive recoil many of us feel to such a challenge generally has little to do with any risk of serious reprisal from the state or even censure from society. Indeed, were we to act in such a fashion, we might well be admired, at least by some. Nevertheless we hesitate, fearing the loss of our cherished privacy, of some of our possessions, of the order and control we seek to bring to our lives. Yet, Maurin insisted, the teaching of Jesus is unequivocal on the point:

"inasmuch as you have done it to the least of these ... you have done it unto me."

Catholic Worker practice of the works of mercy has sometimes involved an admittedly creative reinterpretation of the classic Christian teaching. "Visiting the prisoner" could mean going to jail for an act of conscience. "Instructing the ignorant" could be understood as walking a picket line to protest and bring attention to a social evil. Yet however much their scope might be extended by the Worker, the traditional corporal and spiritual works of mercy have remained throughout the movement's history the very heart of its singular mission and method. They are, as Peter Maurin always stressed, the substance of Catholic Direct Action.

The Question of Violence

Consideration of Direct Action inevitably raises the pivotal question of violence. The common perception, now as ever, is that anarchism is by definition violent, and that, moreover, its violence is of a particularly despicable type: terrorism. Countless political cartoons over the years have portrayed anarchists as dark, "foreign" types with bombs under their greasy overcoats. Such images were vividly impressed on the public mind in the early decades of this century by a number of dramatic events: the attempted murder of Henry Clay Frick, a steel plant manager in Homestead, Pennsylvania, after his private guards (along with state militiamen) fired on strikers; the assassination of President McKinley by self-avowed anarchist Leon Colgosz in 1901; the Wall Street bombing of 1919, in which a good number of clerks, messengers, typists and other ordinary folk were maimed or killed (though no capitalist tycoons — the intended targets of the act — lost their lives).

Despite these and other sensational examples of anarchist "propaganda of the deed," by the end of the First World War most anarchists had rejected such acts as ineffective and counter-productive. Nevertheless, the majority of anarchists continued to consider armed insurrection and defensive violence as justifiable means for furthering or protecting the revolution. On the other hand, a not insignificant minority of anarchists have always been absolute pacifists, rejecting *any* violence or duress as fundamentally contradictory to anarchist principle. As cogently summarized by contemporary British anarchist Donald Rooum, their view is that:

> [T]he revolution can only succeed if it involves no violence whatever. ... [A] society established by violent defeat of the bosses could only be maintained by violent suppression of the ex-bosses. Therefore, violence cannot lead to anarchy, but only to a change of bosses.

For the Catholic Worker, the question of the use of violence is a profoundly theological issue. If even God will not trespass on the awesome gift of human moral freedom (as the Judeo-Christian tradition asserts unequivocally that God will not), then no mere human can presume an authority over another that the Creator does not assert. God operates through self-emptying invitation rather than compulsion, something never more clearly expressed than in Jesus on the cross. Christians, therefore, are called to no less. They can never legitimately impose their will upon, and at the expense of, even the individual human conscience, much less the individual human life. Violence, therefore, is antithetical to the Worker conception of itself as an anarchistic movement. This is because an essential element of its anarchism is a respect for human freedom so absolute as to disallow any coercive action, of which violence is clearly the ultimate and most extreme form.

"Christian Anarchism" — An Oxymoron?

The Catholic Worker's claim to anarchistic credentials has often exasperated traditional philosophical anarchists, who are inclined to argue that the "Christian anarchism" touted by the movement is an oxymoron. A venerable anarchist rallying cry, they point out, was "Neither God nor Master," and the deity affirmed by the Worker as the ultimate ground of its meaning was sometimes scorned as the "tyrant in heaven" by early anarchist polemicists.

Given the sorry history of Christian complicity with oppressive political systems, such an attitude is understandable. While the church began as an illicit cult and was for a time persecuted on the grounds that it was subversive to the state, once it gained legal recognition under Constantine it quickly became the foremost defender of the prerogatives of established power, swathing government in the *imprimatur* of divine authority. Absolute monarchies buttressed their claims with the theological notion of the "divine right of kings." When governments summoned their people to war, the church always managed to find theological justification for the conflict and also for the unlucky citizen's "Christian obligation" to give up his life for the cause of the nation.

Indeed, anarchists argue with some justification, if ecclesiastical history teaches us anything, it is that whenever the church gains power, individual freedom suffers. Calvin's Geneva used the authority of the magistrate to punish those who even dared make jokes about the ordained ministers who ran the community as a theocracy. Through the institution of the "established Church," various Christian communions — not only the Roman — for generations trampled on the rights of conscience of those they labeled heretics. (The pious Puritans of the Massachusetts Colony, for example, themselves refugees from the persecution of the Church of England, saw no inconsistency in executing Quakers and other non-conformists for theological dissent once they held the reins of civil power in the New World.) And, as the ultimate and eternal argument for Christianity's intrinsic hostility to human freedom, there was the Spanish Inquisition.

For turn-of-the-century anarchists in the United States, this long and dismal chronicle was made present and specific in the extensive homiletic promotion monopoly capitalism enjoyed from thousands of middle-class Protestant pulpits across the country. Evangelical pastors were virtually unanimous in their assurance that entrepreneurial success was a sure sign of God's favor. They were united, as well, in their denunciations of radicalism and labor organization as transgressive of the God-given rights of property and the employer. The conventionally pious whispered with virtuous horror over the moral failings of the "under-class" — drink, spousal abuse, illegitimacy — all the while turning a blind eye to the larger systemic injustices upon which their own middle-class probity depended, injustices which were often the cause of the very evils they so self-righteously condemned in the poor.

However, despite the Protestant hegemony in American religious life of the time, it was generally the Roman Catholic Church which, for anarchists, particularly symbolized the ostensibly spiritual despotism against which they rebelled. The Church's very structure — hierarchical, bureaucratic, authoritarian — exemplified everything anarchists opposed. Its nearly unlimited claim to sovereignty over the consciences of its communicants was equally offensive to anarchist conviction.

From the Church's side, the magisterium's animosity toward even relatively moderate liberalism, much less anarchistic radicalism, was equally vehement, perhaps reaching its definitive expression in Pope Pius IX's infamous *Syllabus of Errors* (1864), with its anathematizing of liberalism, rationalism, revolution and democracy. Given all this, it is not surprising that most traditional anarchists have viewed with suspicion, if not outright hostility, Worker claims to be at once Catholic and anarchistic.

As already noted, the Worker's friends in the Church ("especially the bishops") have often had their own misgivings as to the movement's embrace of anarchism. Such hesitations are surely based in significant part upon the awkward fact that — as Mel Piehl notes in *Breaking Bread* — anarchism has no explicit basis in Catholic tradition, unlike other essential Worker concepts such as the Mystical Body or voluntary poverty. In fact, one could go further: Anarchism is directly antagonistic to the Church's conventional teaching that the state and its coercive powers, codified in law, are God's appointed instruments for restraining and, when necessary, punishing the innate sinfulness of fallen humankind.

On this point, some theologians have suggested that anarchism might be a viable model had men and women not rebelled against their Creator. Given the reality of human selfishness and sin, however, unregulated exercise of human freedom will inevitably lead to personal disaster and corporate chaos. Indeed, a primary focus of traditional Christian spiritual discipline — the taming of the unruly human will — is based on an assumption that, left to our own devices, we can only go astray. Thus, according to this conventional view, the exercise of authority by the state and our submission to that authority are necessary accommodations to the reality of the fall.

Christian anarchists respond to such arguments with the observation that the venerable Christian doctrine of the fall applies to *all* human beings, those who govern as well as those governed. Just as the ruled bear the wound of sin, so do the rulers. Just as the subject will at times use freedom unwisely or malevolently, so will the sovereign. In fact, given the self-evident reality that "power corrupts," those who claim authority can be expected to act out the consequences of their brokenness even more perniciously than those over whom they wield that authority.

In short, the Christian anarchist contends, the universal effect of the fall means not that the limitation of human freedom is necessary or desirable, but quite the opposite: that the expansion of liberty is a positive spiritual good. The larger the scope allowed for freedom, the greater the chance of making possible some measure of justice and wholeness in human affairs. Liberty, whatever its risks, ensures at least the opportunity for full exercise of that mature responsibility for one's choices and actions which should be the mark of a man or woman made in the image of God. As Peter Maurin was fond of repeating: "the best organization is self-organization."

Having said all that, the Christian anarchist must admit that the majority opinion in Scripture — at least as traditionally interpreted — appears to come down heavily on the side of coercive human authority in all its forms. Along with a disturbingly placid acceptance of slavery and patriarchy, the Bible in general appears to hold human government, no matter how despotic, in rather remarkably high regard. The authors of the Book of Judges speak with dismay of those times when there was "no king in Israel and each man did as seemed right in his own eyes." St. Peter encourages Christians to "honor the Emperor." St. Paul declares explicitly that *all* human government is "ordained by God," that tax collectors are doing God's work, and that rebellion against civil authority is rebellion against God.

Making allowance for the fact of St. Paul's rather conspicuous bias in favor of authority of all kinds (Ammon Hennacy could never forgive him for telling slaves to obey their masters), there is also the fact that even Jesus himself instructed inquirers to "render unto Caesar that which is Caesar's" (without granting to Caesar the right to define what is legitimately his — a point often overlooked by those manipulating this particular teaching in the interest of the state's ever-expanding claims).

Despite what might appear to be a monolithic biblical perspective on the subject, Christian anarchists are nevertheless able to find support, both in Scripture and tradition, for their own negative judgment upon the imposed authority of the state.

In the first place, exegetes have long recognized that, alongside Old Testament propaganda on behalf of the Davidic dynasty and its prerogatives, there also exists in the text a strong counter-stream of opposition to monarchical claims. When Yahweh God establishes the

Hebrew people in the promised land according to tribes, there is no provision for a central government or a sovereign — for the simple reason that Yahweh, through local judges, is to be the ruler of the chosen people. When a later generation begins to clamor for a king, it is specifically noted that these demands are based upon a desire to be "like the other nations," which is precisely what Yahweh has consistently insisted the Hebrew people are *not* intended to be. When God acquiesces and sends the prophet Samuel to anoint Saul (and later David), this acceptance of a monarchy is clearly treated as an accommodation to the nation's sin.

As for the New Testament witness, it cannot escape notice that the same Paul of Tarsus who rather grandly assures his readers in the Epistle to the Romans that the righteous have nothing to fear from the power of the state is the Paul who, according to Christian tradition, was beheaded under Roman law for his unstinting preaching of the gospel. St. Peter, too, lost his life in Roman persecution of the apostolic church. Even more significant is the example of Christ himself, who in freely following his destiny became a victim of both the religious and political powers of his day.

In the last book of the canonical New Testament, the Revelation to Saint John, Christian anarchists find even more explicit evidence for a stream of "counter-tradition" on the question of human government. In the Apocalypse, the state — under the figure of the Roman empire, the paramount form of government in the writer's day — is portrayed as nothing less than the literal embodiment of the spirit of Anti-Christ. Its economically-based pretensions to absolute supremacy are represented (and ruthlessly caricatured) in the vivid imagery of Babylon, the Great Whore, through which evil incarnate exercises its oppressive sway over humankind, making the "whole world drunk with her debaucheries."

While a current and widely popular Protestant school of interpretation consigns the "events" of the Revelation to a specific "end times" at the climax of history, thereby rendering them to all intents and purposes irrelevant (except as some sort of gaudy, futuristic *roman a clef*), this is far from the only legitimate way of reading the text. The historic Christian understanding has always been that *all* time after the triumph of the cross and until the consummation of history is, in fact, the "end times." Seen in this light, the extraordinary images of the Apocalypse can be understood not as predictions of some future catastrophe, but rather as symbolic depictions of ongoing spiritual realities continually in operation as elements of the existential condition of the human race.

Under such an interpretation, a fundamental message of the sacred text would be that nation and state are, by their very nature, masks for the demonic. This would be true not only of one particular government — whether in the future (as fundamentalist Protestants believe) or in the past (as the majority of liberal exegetes, Catholic and Protestant alike, suggest). It would be true of *all* governments — even the most apparently benign or well-intentioned. On this point, it is surely significant that when the Tempter, in the Gospel of Luke, shows Jesus "all the kingdoms of the world in a moment" and offers him their power in exchange for blasphemous worship, Jesus does not contradict Satan's rather astounding assertion that full authority in these earthly realms is his and he gives it to whomever he pleases, nor does the text seem to imply that such a claim is anything other than the plain truth. If this is the case, then the Christian — always understood to be a member of a new "race," the Body of Christ, and a citizen of a new Kingdom, that of the Risen Lord — can legitimately assert a freedom from the dominion of the governing authorities of this world on the basis of a claim to prior and quite contrary allegiance. As St. Peter told the authorities of his day: "We must obey God rather than men."

Reflection on the Gospel eventually led the church to an understanding that slavery is an affront to the God-given nature of the human person and thus a grave moral evil. Christians arrived at this conviction despite Scriptural evidences of acceptance and even tacit endorsement of slavery (Paul's returning of the runaway slave Onesimus to his owner, Philemon, was another thing that outraged Ammon Hennacy). Similarly, the Christian anarchist would argue, it is possible to claim a legitimate place for anarchism within the Christian tradition (and a home for Christians within anarchism), even in the face of the Scriptural and historical evidence of tolerance and even embrace of the coercive instruments of what the church once called "the temporal power." Perhaps, in time, the Christian anarchist position will no longer seem anomalous — any more than Christian opposition to slavery seems contradictory to us today. The saints, after all, have in many instances lived out just such anarchism on a practical level — one thinks of St. Francis flouting the foreign policy of the state by going personally to visit the enemy Sultan in the middle of a war.

Just as the philosophical anarchist opposes civil authority on the basis of essential human freedom, so the Christian anarchist declares his or her independence from the constraining institutions of society in the name of what St. Paul terms the "glorious liberty of the children of God." As is true with philosophical anarchism, however, such liberty is decidedly not self-serving license. Indeed, for the Christian anarchist, the fundamental prerequisite for emancipation from the strictures of spurious human authority is submission to the authentic authority of God. Since God is, by essential nature, self-emptying love, submission to divine authority means living in accord with the reality of such love. It means having that law of love written on our hearts and in our minds. It means giving flesh and substance to that love through our actions. The Christian's call to submission in freedom requires taking personal responsibility for bringing God's love into play in the immediacy of our world.

Thus, Christian anarchism, like Christian personalism, is at its heart a summons to begin to live intentionally, to strive to enflesh the true nature of reality so as to make justice, freedom, security and love present for all God's children. Rather than sloughing off this responsibility onto institutions, nations, or bureaucracies, Christian anarchists insist that we can and must claim it for ourselves as the true measure of our freedom in Christ. In so doing, we undermine the domination of Babylon the Great simply by living out the Gospel as if Babylon's overweening authority did not exist. We can dare to choose such freedom because we believe that the day will come when, in fact, Babylon will no longer exist, when we and all of redeemed humanity will join the jubilant shout of the Revelation: "Babylon is fallen! Babylon is fallen! The kingdoms of this world are become the realm of our God and of God's Messiah!"

Yet we must always be careful, as Dorothy Day was keenly aware, not to project all of Babylon's power outside of ourselves, whether onto other people or onto the larger institutions of society. If the principle of rebellion against reality — which is the fundamental definition of evil — is at the core of Babylon's meaning, then that principle lives not only in external structures and oppressive classes but also within our own hearts, our own motives, our own intentional communities. Indeed, probably no one needs to be more mindful of the pervasive reach of sin than the one who would presume to act in the name of that personal responsibility which is the essential consequence of anarchistic freedom.

Nevertheless, if through hesitancy over our own brokenness, fear of possible consequences or simple complacency we refuse the weighty gift of our liberty, we risk giving the lie to the transcending reality we profess. As Peter Maurin wrote:

In the first centuries
of Christianity
the hungry were fed
at a personal sacrifice,
the naked were clothed
at a personal sacrifice,
the homeless were sheltered
at a personal sacrifice.
And because the poor
were fed, clothed and sheltered
at a personal sacrifice,
the pagans used to say
about the Christians
"See how they love each other."
In our own day
the poor are no longer
fed, clothed and sheltered
at a personal sacrifice
but at the expense of the taxpayers.
And because the poor
are no longer
fed, clothed and sheltered
at a personal sacrifice,
the pagans say about the
Christians
"See how they pass the buck."

Catholic Worker Anarchism

Even within the movement itself, there has always been considerable divergence of opinion regarding the meaning of Catholic Worker anarchism and its place within the larger whole of the "Worker idea." On one hand, some Workers consider anarchism to be a crucial and defining principle of the movement's vision. This is particularly true of those inspired by the model of Ammon Hennacy, who proudly labeled himself a Christian anarchist both before, during and after his direct participation in the New York community. On the opposite side of the question are those individuals — or, in a few instances, entire Worker houses — which have repudiated anarchism altogether. Falling somewhere between these two positions are perhaps the majority of Catholic Workers both past and present, many of whom would probably hold a view similar to that articulated by one long-time member of the present Los Angeles community: "We are not anarchists; we're *anarchistic*."

There can be no question that Dorothy Day herself was an anarchist all her adult life. In a 1967 tribute to *Daily Worker* columnist Mike Gold, an old friend from her early radical days on the Lower East Side, Day commented that she had been "an anarchist then as I am now." Nevertheless, in the mid 1970s she told an interviewer from within the movement that she preferred the label "personalist communitarian" over "anarchist." Whether this was due to the former term's resonance with language customarily used by Peter Maurin or to the negative connotations "anarchist" held for many of the Worker's supporters in the Church is difficult to assess. In either case, Day's hesitations as to the expediency of an anarchist identification for herself or the Worker movement are presumably what lay behind the almost apologetic note she once struck in discussing Ammon Hennacy's voluble anarchism. When Ammon spoke of being an anarchist, she wrote, what he was "really" talking about was "fighting the modern state and war." (That Hennacy himself would have accepted so circumscribed an interpretation of his passionate commitment to anarchistic self-direction seems unlikely.)

Despite Day's occasional attempts to mitigate the potential offense of the Worker's anarchistic convictions, William Miller surely overstates the matter when he writes in his biography that "Dorothy would have nothing to do with the anarchist label. ..." In fact, as Miller notes elsewhere, Day didn't particularly like *any* limiting label being applied to her — whether "anarchist," "distributist" or "saint" (on this last, her comment was that she refused to be "dismissed so easily"). If "anarchist" carried with it too many confusing connotations, she was not adverse to choosing less threatening terminology to convey her beliefs, especially when that terminology could be traced directly to Maurin. Nevertheless, she "wish[ed] people would not be so afraid of words." Anarchism, albeit of a somewhat idiosyncratic sort, would remain a part of Worker theory and action, no matter what vocabulary might be used to describe it.

The thorny issue of anarchism's place in the "Worker idea" was further complicated by the fact that, however deep her philosophical commitment to anarchism in principle, Dorothy Day had a personality which tended toward the dictatorial in practice. (Evelyn Waugh described her — after they met over a long lunch — as an "autocratic saint.") While quick to condemn the imposition of power in political, bureaucratic or institutional contexts, Day showed little hesitation about asserting her own authority within the Worker when she felt the occasion required it. Throughout the mid-to-late 1930s, she — and, to all intents and purposes, she alone — determined the contents of *The Catholic Worker*, considering herself to be, as she put it in one instance, both "editor and censor." Even after she began appointing "Managing Editors" in the 1940s, she was still very much in control. She blocked the publication of articles with which she disagreed. She personally edited others, on at least one occasion replacing part of a submission with something she liked better from another source — without notice to or permission from the credited author. Perhaps most importantly, she set the tone of the paper through the inclusion in each issue of her own, often lengthy, column.

In the early years of the movement, Day also exercised considerable influence in the setting up of new Catholic Worker communities around the country. Typically, being informed that a "cell" of *Catholic Worker* readers was interested in opening its own House of Hospitality, she would visit the group and then, after consultation, name one of its members the "Director" of the new venture, thereby providing a kind of "apostolic succession."

Once a Worker house was established, however, Day generally insisted upon its autonomy, both from the New York community and from her own oversight, refusing to become personally involved in its affairs. As she wrote to the leader of one faction-ridden house who had sent her a letter seeking definitive guidance on a local dispute: "You will have to work it out for yourselves." On the other hand, on one occasion in 1946 she "officially disbanded" the Boston Catholic Worker after that community deposed a Director of whom she approved.

In the New York community, Day's dominance was an unquestioned fact of life, not only through the considerable force of her personality but also, upon occasion, through her own highly effective (but seemingly far from anarchistic) forms of Direct Action. When a cabal of young Workers in the early years pushed for eliminating the "dead wood" of men from the street who were unlikely candidates for understanding and implementing the lofty goals of the personalist revolution, Day saw to it that the insurgents were soon gone — and did so despite Maurin's proposal that he and she simply leave the house to the dissenters and start the work over again somewhere else.

Similarly, when a group of young people in the 1960s began cohabiting in Worker housing in violation of traditional Catholic moral teaching, Day unilaterally made the decision to stop paying rent on the apartments they occupied. And, as already noted, when a feisty group of young Workers became involved in publishing a literary journal she found offensive, Dorothy rose up in wrath and expelled the youthful iconoclasts from the community, prompting the following impudent but telling riposte:

> [Four] staff members of the Catholic Worker were stomped off the Worker set as a result of publishing in *Fuck You*, a Magazine of the Arts, or as a result of continued association with its editor. This outburst ... seems to us not in the spirit of anarchy. ... However, we understand the need of the grand old lady of pacifism for a closed metaphysical system where there are no disturbances, such as *Fuck You*, a Magazine of the Arts. Therefore, in future issues of this magazine we shall refrain from any mention of the Catholic Worker to save Miss Day from any more metaphysical distress.

That Day knew well the distress, metaphysical and otherwise, that the life she had chosen could occasion is well documented in her journals. At least some of this distress appears to have resulted from the fact that, while she was temperamentally a leader, she was never entirely comfortable in that role due to the anarchistic theory to which she ascribed — or at least aspired. While referring to herself in a 1939 letter to a priest as being "in command" of the Worker (hardly an anarchistic notion), she also wrote on another occasion that "I am ... in the position of a dictator trying to legislate himself out of existence."

Day assumed leadership because circumstances, her own character, and the clarity of her vision for the movement thrust leadership upon her. In many instances, those who joined the Worker (the "young people," as she came to refer to them in her later years) not only submitted to that leadership but also became overly dependent upon it, much to Day's exasperation, since she hoped for them the same personalist responsibility for self-direction that she accepted for herself. On other occasions, whether through anarchistic principle or the working out of unresolved private agendas, some of these young people opposed her, resented her, and left the movement grumbling about the inconsistencies between its professed anarchism and the reality of its daily life. The results of Day's ongoing personal struggle between natural leadership and a philosophical need to divest herself of "command" may not have always conformed to the high standards of anarchist theory, but that struggle assured that the core values she had received from Peter Maurin would remain central to the movement's theory and practice.

While it is clear that Dorothy Day and Ammon Hennacy were both anarchists, the question of whether Peter Maurin's "scheme" (as he once termed it) was explicitly anarchistic is somewhat more problematic. One searches the "Easy Essays" in vain for any reference to anarchism, although Maurin does from time to time quote individual anarchists favorably. Given his tendency to selective use of his sources, however, such citations cannot, in and of themselves, prove Maurin would have defined himself as a philosophical anarchist.

Ammon Hennacy told the story that, after hearing Peter Maurin speak at Milwaukee's Holy Family Catholic Worker House in the late 1930s, he commented that Maurin "talk[ed] like an anarchist," to which Maurin purportedly replied, "Sure I am an anarchist. All thinking people are anarchists. But I prefer the name 'personalist.'" While this story may well have a basis in fact, the words Hennacy puts in Maurin's mouth sound remarkably like Ammon and hardly anything at all like Peter. (It is difficult to imagine the irenic Maurin using a divisive term like "all thinking people.") Nonetheless, it does not seem unlikely that — however much he may have embraced anarchistic theory — Maurin would have subsumed it under the more inclusive (and less intimidating) designation of personalism. Dorothy Day said as much when, in a reminiscence written after Maurin's death, she noted that "Peter did not want to be fragmented by being labeled. . . . anarchist. First of all, we are Catholics."

Along with "personalist," the other term Maurin favored for himself and his revolution was "communitarian." As he wrote in one of the "Essays":

A communitarian
is a fellow
who refuses to be
what the other fellow is
and tries to be
what he wants
[the other fellow]
to be.
A communitarian revolution
is basically a
personal revolution.
It starts with I,
not with Them.

Certainly in its spirit, if not all its ideological specifics, such a "personal revolution" would be profoundly anarchistic. Maurin himself lived as a practical anarchist, doing what he felt called to do "on his own responsibility," without sanction of the state or any other authority. A serious (and seditious) anarchistic insight underlies the superficial tautology of his maxim that:

If everybody
organized himself,
everybody would
be organized.

If everybody truly "organized himself," of course, there would be little need for the over-arching structures of government and bureaucracy, a fact Maurin referenced more explicitly when he wrote that we must "look ... to the individual, not to the state, for the solution of social problems."

William Miller comments in *A Harsh and Dreadful Love*, somewhat in passing, that Maurin called himself an anarchist upon various occasions, but gives no specifics beyond Hennacy's story. Whether or not, in fact, Maurin considered anarchism a part of his program, there are numerous clear parallels between his Christian personalism and traditional anarchistic theory. Both affirm the fundamental priority of personal responsibility, which presumes the necessity of personal freedom. Both are suspicious of the state and its attempts to impose order from above, contending that fruitful social forms can only "trickle up" from below. Both embrace voluntary cooperativism as the best functional model for human organization. Both stress the importance of Direct Action for change.

In considering the relationship between Worker personalism and anarchism, it is striking that a statement of "Beliefs and Values" developed by various Catholic Worker houses during the late 1980s and early 1990s merges personalism and anarchism into one single principle. First published in 1991 in the *Catholic Agitator*, the monthly publication of the Los Angeles community, this section reads:

> PERSONALISM/ANARCHISM: We believe that we have a personal responsibility to care for those in need. We do not look to any state authority to do this work or to approve the work we do. We do not receive a salary, nor do we accept government money or non-profit status to do that which Jesus Christ calls us to do.

Rejection of the "Bureaucratic Principle"

Even to the not so casual observer, it might sometimes seem that the primary evidence of anarchism in any Catholic Worker community is a determined unprofessionalism, a kind of seat-of-the-pants, *ad hoc* improvisational approach that intentionally seeks (as Piehl nicely terms it) a kind of "anti-bureaucratic formlessness." This extemporaneous method is not based on any sense that the poor should be willing to make do with casual, unthinking, or slipshod efforts on their behalf, as in the hideous maxim "beggars can't be choosers." Rather, it grows from a conviction that long-range, elaborately structured schemes for social service inevitably become inflexible, devoting more energy, finally, to the perpetuation of their own programs and prerogatives than to the needs of those they were created to serve. The regulations and consistency required for the functioning of complex systems make it difficult, if not impossible, for one to act spontaneously and directly within them to meet the unique human dimensions of particular need.

Further, the more complicated the organization, the more it distances the person serving from the person being served. The buffers of bureaucracy not only allow but even require a kind of psychological and spiritual anonymity. The "provider" is reduced to his or her function ("I don't make the rules"). The recipient loses personal specificity and becomes a "case."

What some have called the "bureaucratic principle" inevitably requires uniformity, depersonalization (often in the name of "professionalism") and top-heavy administrative structures. There is a profound spiritual difference between the bureaucrat's "I can give you a voucher" and the personalist's "Come home with me." In that difference lies the ultimate significance of Catholic Workers' ongoing efforts at simple, direct responses to the needs of the poor among whom they live and serve. As is often pointed out in the movement, a primary goal of the personalist revolution must always be the recovery of that "I-thou" connection between individuals of which philosopher/theologian Martin Buber writes so compellingly out of his Jewish tradition. In this "I-thou" interaction, the authentic personhood of one reveals itself in honesty and vulnerability to the personhood of another, accepting and loving that other as an image of God in his or her own right, worthy of full attention and care. In light of such an aim, a conscious repudiation of the bureaucratic principle is clearly the necessary first step toward a more human model of service.

Worker Anarchism in Practice

How far any particular Catholic Worker community goes in the direction of a "free anarchist commune," as Piehl terms it, depends upon not only the convictions but also, no doubt, the personality types of the individuals involved. Nonetheless, most Worker houses do operate on the basis of certain shared principles which could, at least loosely, be termed anarchistic.

To begin with, each person who joins in the work of a house is understood to be acting on his or her own responsibility. No one should or can be compelled to become or, more importantly, *remain* a Catholic Worker. A constant theme in many communities over the years has been the importance of willing, voluntary participation, with the corollary freedom of any member to leave at any time (no matter how great the continuing need) rather than remain out of a sense of obligation, external expectation or guilt. There is considerable divergence within the movement, however, as to whether a community exercises some level of "screening" of potential members or simply accepts anyone proposing to join it. As noted earlier, the original New York Worker clearly exemplified the latter approach. As Dorothy Day explained in her 1939 book *House of Hospitality*:

> ... we take whoever comes to us as sent by God and do not believe in picking and choosing. If we start eliminating then there is no end to it. Everyone wishes to eliminate someone else.

Despite this precedent, other more recent Worker communities have — often on the basis of bitter experience — become somewhat more selective about whom they will welcome as a community member.

Unlike traditional religious orders, the movement has always eschewed a novitiate, a normative rule or vows. Therefore, most communities have been exceedingly relaxed regarding any particular individual's extent of participation, length of stay or personal acceptance of all aspects of the "Worker idea." This still holds true to a significant degree, although in a number of Worker houses there are certain agreed expectations regarding some sort of "bottom-line" involvement in the community's activities and at least short-term time commitments.

As to formation, people are drawn to the Worker for a variety of reasons and with widely varying levels of understanding of its principles. While ongoing "clarification of thought" — through informal discussion around the chopping block as much as through formal presentations — is in itself a kind of formation, most communities have declined to set up structured procedures for "indoctrination," a word Maurin often used in a positive sense. More recently, however, recognizing how profoundly our perceptions and sensibilities are molded by the inescapable contemporary culture (the values and assumptions of which are at such variance with Catholic Worker thought), some communities have embarked on more intentional processes of formation, including regular Bible study and what one community terms "cultural critique."

"Leadership" and Decision-Making

For any group attempting to function on anarchistic principle, the question of how it arrives at the decisions that will determine its character, common activities and interrelationships must loom large.

Traditional anarchism generally allows for two different but equally acceptable methods for decision-making, the first of which is spontaneous, task-specific, non-compulsory leadership. While the notion of anarchistic "leadership" may sound in and of itself contradictory, the fact is that anarchists have no intrinsic objection to organizers or leaders, so long as compliance with their direction is strictly voluntary.

As outlined by Donald Rooum, such leadership is a matter of an individual deciding independently to take responsibility for doing something and then soliciting others — by either invitation or example — to join in the effort if they are so inclined. With his distaste for any organization but "self-organization," Peter Maurin's preference clearly lay with this extraordinarily fluid strategy — indeed, he even opposed organizational *meetings*. His own option, as already noted, was the power of personal example: He would break rocks and those who, in the exercise of their personal freedom, chose to join him in the work would do so. Eventually, the road would be built.

This was also the approach exemplified by Dorothy Day. She simply started *The Catholic Worker* and then welcomed those who came to join her in publishing it and living out the life of service its message proposed. Such precedents ensured that this sort of charismatic leadership became the initial norm for the movement and it continues to be the pattern followed in the New York community, among a number of others. In these Worker houses, the view tends to be that "natural" leadership will emerge when required through an organic process of discernment which, while difficult to formulate, still serves the movement well even after the loss of the defining presence of Dorothy Day.

The alternative anarchistic approach to decision making utilizes some form of consensus, whether formal or informal. This method too has influenced many Catholic Worker communities, especially through the notable example of the American Friends Service Committee, which by its practice brought consensus models to the attention of the Vietnam era anti-war movement. Indeed, over the last twenty-five years, some form of consensus has gradually become the practice of the majority of — though far from all — Catholic Worker communities.

It is important to stress that true consensus is not, even by default, majority rule. If the majority "rules," then a minority is losing, which can only lead to power blocks, interest groups, splintering of community and the coercive imposition of power, all of which are at war with anarchistic freedom, the dignity of conscience and, ultimately, the common good. As Peter Maurin stated unequivocally: "I do not believe in majority rule. I do not believe in having meetings and elections ... people [being] divided into factions."

This repudiation of majority rule may offend us — accustomed as we are to the notion that representative democracy and its mechanisms are the highest form of human organization. And the fact is that consensus is very hard work — hard because we must so value human freedom, even in the context of necessarily corporate endeavors, that we will choose not to move forward until a way has been found to meet every individual's concerns on the issue at hand. Then, and only then, can all work together in true unity toward a common goal.

Such a method might well seem impossible by any normal standard of human behavior. When we honestly believe we are right, when we are convinced that the general good can best (perhaps only) be served by one particular course of action, it is difficult to continue searching for an alternative, creative way to proceed so as to incorporate a perspective that may seem to us staggeringly off point. It is here that a Christian's practice of consensus has something beyond the "normal standard" to draw upon: the Gospel principle of "mutual submission in love." As Dorothy Day once wrote in the context of an article on "Holy Obedience":

> Philosophical anarchism ... requires that we follow the Gospel precept to be obedient to every living thing: "Be subject therefore to every human creature for God's sake."

While such a sentiment would likely make many a philosophical anarchist's hair stand on end, it points to a penetrating spiritual and psychological truth. If, in the name of love for another, we chose willingly to submit to his or her needs or convictions — at real cost to our own opinions or desires — then we have exercised our liberty in the most profound way possible. This holds true even in explicitly coercive situations, as Jesus makes clear in his teaching that, if someone forces us to march one mile, we should accompany him two, that if someone takes our coat, we should give our shirt also. By going beyond the demand made, we suddenly turn the situation around. Through our very submission beyond what is demanded, we regain "control" of our actions and so live out the reality of our existential freedom.

On the level of Christian community, if truly *mutual* submission in love is realized, then the intentions of consensus can begin to be fulfilled in the context of the transforming work of the Spirit in the Mystical Body of Christ. This is because, given the reality of our selfishness and ego, not to mention our legitimately differing views and needs, the only effective means for achieving genuine consensus are mutual forbearance, self-sacrifice, and a movement from self-interest to that self-emptying love modeled perfectly by God's love for us in Christ. And it is just this sort of love, Maurin taught, that is the life-blood of authentic personalist community.

To trust ourselves to so arduous a process as this, we must be willing to "waste" time in order that our hearts and the hearts of others might be moved to new understanding and deeper insight. We must be willing to admit that even when we are most passionately certain we are right, there may be truth that we have not considered, some alternative course that should be explored. We must believe that God is mysteriously at work in others even when they are most annoyingly at odds with the clarity of our own perspective. We must, finally, care more that the other's concerns find a place in the ultimate decision than that our own point of view prevail.

A twenty-five year veteran of the present Los Angeles house notes in this regard that a habitual weakness of Catholic Worker consensus methods has been a tendency to overlook those psychological dimensions — unstated agendas, unresolved personal issues, "personality quirks" — that must inevitably play a part in the process. These realities require acknowledgment, he argues, or they will derail any attempts at genuinely consensual community. Such matters must be named and, as much as possible, separated from conviction and proposals for action — despite the current truism that ideology is always a creature of personality. It does not require great imagination to recognize that such introspective insight requires not only substantial effort but also considerable maturity.

The demanding requirements of authentic consensus are, of course, completely contrary to our modern Western focus on the end result, on productivity and efficiency. Such a vision of human interaction presumes that no person is so unimportant that he can be ignored or trampled over. No one can be treated as a means to an end, because every person is an end in and of herself. The ultimate goal — whether we call it the revolution or the Kingdom of God — must be able to be enfleshed *now*, in this moment, between us, or we can never claim its viability for some future utopia. Indeed, *only* what works "now" will lead us to "then." Any method which would dismiss the importance of the individual person in the interest of some future good is unworthy of that Eternal Reign which is the only future of which we can be certain, and which is therefore the standard by which all that comes before it must be judged.

A Sublime Paradox

The theological meaning of Catholic Worker anarchism was perhaps best articulated in an essay of Dorothy Day's first published in the Spring of 1970:

> . ... St. Paul defined the Catholic Worker's idea of anarchism, the positive word, by saying of the followers of Jesus, "For such there is no law." Those who have given up all idea of domination and power and the manipulation of others are "not under the law."... For those who live in Christ Jesus, for those who have "put on Christ," for those who have washed the feet of others, there is no law. They have the liberty of the children of God.

Day's stirring depiction of Christian freedom, a freedom that finds its definitive expression not in self-assertion but in humble service, notably fails to address the question of whether those who have *not* "given up all idea of domination and power and the manipulation of others" would be best served by an anarchist social order. On this point, she follows the path laid out by Peter Maurin, who taught that we should simply begin "living as we want the other fellow to live," rather than attempting to impose our vision for society on those not yet ready to embrace that vision's lofty ideals.

Especially significant in this passage is Day's reference to the "washing of feet." This image, taken from an episode recorded only in St. John's Gospel, is a recurrent theme in Day's discussions of anarchism as understood and practiced by the Worker: Jesus, at the Last Supper, strips to his tunic and moves among his disciples, performing the customary servant's role of washing their dusty feet.

In 1972, reflecting on Peter Maurin's anarchism, she wrote:

> [It] was on one level based on [the] principle of subsidiarity [that governments should never do what small bodies can accomplish], and on a higher level on that scene at the Last Supper where Christ washed the feet of His Apostles. He came to serve, to show the new Way, the way of the powerless. In the face of Empire, the Way of Love.

On another occasion, writing for the Catholic journal *Ave Maria*, she was drawn yet again to the compelling figure of the incarnate God on his knees with a towel around his waist, doing the work of the lowliest of household servants:

> Philosophical anarchism ... requires that we ... [wash] the feet of others, as Jesus did at the Last Supper. "You call me Master and Lord," He said, "and rightly so, for that is what I am. Then if I, your Lord, have washed your feet, you also ought to wash one another's feet. I have set you an example; you are to do as I have done for you." To serve others, not to seek power over them. Not to dominate, not to judge others.

This haunting image of enacted "servant love" captures more powerfully than any theoretical articulation the unique nature of the Christian anarchism espoused by the Catholic Worker.

In one of her "On Pilgrimage" columns, Dorothy explained that anarchism in another way, playing off St. Augustine's famous adage: "To us at the Catholic Worker, anarchism means 'Love God and do as you wish.'" Of course, for the Christian, to truly love God is to wish to follow God's will, not one's own. So, in the end — if Day's statement is to be taken seriously — Catholic Worker anarchism is a sublime paradox: In the name of absolute freedom, we must voluntarily renounce that freedom for the will of God and the common good, becoming the servant of all. We must become like Christ, washing feet at the Last Supper. And, in so doing, we will discover for the first time the true meaning of our freedom.

Chapter Four

Peter Maurin's Green Revolution

While the personalist call is profoundly individual, with each of us meeting God and the meaning of history in the specificity of immediate choice, the ultimate goal of Maurin's vision reached beyond the individual to the larger common good and a more truly human society. Indeed, Maurin sometimes referred to the Catholic Worker as a "Common Good movement," noting that "a person cannot serve God without serving the Common Good." In another of his "Essays," he described his social program as "Catholic communism," which he then went on to identify with "the Common Good doctrine of St. Thomas More, St. Thomas Aquinas and the first Christians."

This collective, social dimension to personalism certainly did not originate with Maurin. As developed by Mounier and Maritain, personalism was from its inception clearly distinct from traditional pietism (of either the Catholic or Protestant varieties) and its inward focus on *my* spiritual growth, *my* relationship with God (or, more recently, *my* psychological integration). While not discounting the need for all of these things, personalism views true internal growth and integration as, by their very nature, making us more fit to be active participants in redemptive history, which has to do not only with the salvation of souls but also the remaking of *every* element of the wounded creation, including human society.

For a Christian personalist such as Maurin — grounded in the fact of the Mystical Body and committed to voluntary communalism and Direct Action on one's own responsibility — the common good could never be imposed by force from "above." It must flower from "below," from individual decisions to live the reality of the new order in faithfulness and hope. In this view, Maurin was clearly a quintessential anarchist, whether he identified himself as such or not.

Maurin made a distinction between the "red revolution" of the Marxists, with its embrace of violence, class warfare, and the tyrannical "dictatorship of the proletariat," and his own "green revolution" which would be effected not by force or coercion but by the power of example leading to *metanoia* and consensual changes in the way people live.

The result of such a "green revolution" would be a society standing in stark contrast to both the monopolistic capitalism of the democracies and the compulsory statist collectivism of the Soviet model:

The Catholic Worker
stands for cooperativism
against capitalism ...
personalism
against socialism. ...
The new order ...
will be functional
not acquisitive;
personalist,
not socialist;
communitarian,
not collectivist;
organismic [*sic*],
not mechanistic.

Contrary to traditional revolutionary rhetoric, according to which old structures must be torn down and smashed to make way for a new, more just world, Maurin, like the Wobblies he and Dorothy Day so much admired, looked to "building the new in the shell of the old," confident that the old order would eventually collapse by itself from the weight of its own contradictions and sin. Until that inevitable collapse, Maurin taught, the job of the personalist is to be busy living the new, approaching order in the midst of the old, trusting in a kind of contagion of love to create changed hearts and redeemed actions which will result in an ever-widening scope for the Eternal Reign of God that is at once with us, in us and still to come.

During the first years of the movement, in the depths of the Great Depression, the Worker — like most of the left of the time — was convinced that this collapse of the present failing system was imminent. Early Worker writings sometimes appear to anticipate that the new organism of Maurin's green revolution will spread relatively rapidly (one is reminded of St. Paul's assurances to his converts that they would see the Second Coming in their own lifetimes). Given the devastating social upheavals of the period, this embrace of human time-frames is perhaps understandable.

Now, however, nearly sixty-five years later, with the predicted collapse and subsequent renewal yet to arrive, we witness Western society going hell-bent in quite the opposite direction: distraction from the authentic human quest by way of consumption and media addiction, ever greater consolidation of wealth in the hands of the few, a consequent shrinking of the middle class and widening of the gap between rich and poor, and an unabashed, philosophically-buttressed rejection of compassion and our essential interconnectedness within the commonweal.

Considering all this, is Maurin's green revolution just one more exercise in wishful utopian thinking? Are the over six decades of Worker action and witness based on his vision no more than a noble experiment that failed? Viewed from our limited Western understanding of time, it would perhaps seem so.

But it can be argued — and the Worker would certainly so argue — that when we touch reality, we begin to see time differently. Time as we experience it is discovered to be a movement toward eternity, an eternity which is at once outside of time and yet present in and "parallel" with it. In the context of eternity, those actions which are faithful to reality — whatever their result in the immediacy of our time — bridge the gap from time to eternity, and it is in eternity that their significance is to be judged. This is not just because their "success" will only be manifest in the blazing clarity of reality washed clean of the brokenness and limitations with which our time is blinded; it is because, viewed with the eye of faith, right now, *in* time, these actions partake of the solidity of eternity, of that which will last forever and against which the things our world holds up as real are seen as insubstantial and transitory ghosts.

In the light of eternity, there is such a thing as "holy failure," failure that is willing to embrace a new value system in which the determinative issue is not immediate results or quick changes, either in an individual or in society, but rather patient, ongoing faithfulness to reality.

Such stubborn faithfulness turns our attention and our hope from fantasies of massive institutional change (and our own potentially heroic role in such change) to something at once more demanding and more within our reach: this moment, this person, this exchange, as we affirm that the whole human story is wrapped up in them.

It should be stressed that this does not mean we are simply to disregard as beyond our individual purview the larger evils of institutions and social systems. The Worker stands in diametrical opposition to the pietist heresy that has allowed American evangelical Christians by and large to turn inward and ignore the structural sins in which they are inextricably entangled and by which they all too often benefit. Prophetic witness against institutional evil is indeed required, both in word and deed, and the Worker has a long history of such witness, borne at often significant personal cost. Yet even as we stand boldly against what St. Paul termed the "principalities and powers," we must always, at the same time, accept personal responsibility to act on the truth in our present particular circumstances, whether or not institutional change is ever effected, doing so in the conviction that any authentic action for love or justice or healing, however small it might seem, has eternal resonance in its own right.

Such a perspective could well seem to place an overpowering, indeed debilitating, weight on the daily interactions of our lives. Yet, amazingly, in the teaching of Jesus such an attitude is seen as the key to a liberating freedom ("sufficient for the day are the troubles thereof"; "take no thought for the morrow"). If we respond to this present moment, whatever its particulars, with self-emptying love, then we will discover that all is there: creation, the kingdom, the new heaven and earth. All these things await us here and now, asking us to dare to take responsibility, to *choose* to see them and, having seen, live by their truth in the reckless freedom of the children of God.

Cult, Culture and Cultivation

With his love of a catchy phrase, Peter Maurin summed up the goal of the green revolution as the creation of a society founded upon and unified by three things: "cult, culture and cultivation." In such a society, he believed, it would truly be "easier for people to be good" because such a social construct would lead men and women back to their fundamental inter-connectedness and grounding in God (through cult), would ensure the flowering of their full intellectual and creative potential (through culture), and would reconnect them with their essential calling to be vicars of God's natural bounty (through cultivation).

The alliterative glibness of "cult, culture and cultivation," redolent as it is of the 1920s advertising sensibility so much a part of Maurin's teaching method, should not obscure the richness and wide-ranging sweep of his vision for a recreated social order. All the defining elements of Worker life and practice — the works of mercy, voluntary poverty, prophetic action against the dominant culture — were for Maurin not only good, necessary and complete in and of themselves, they were also (and continue to be for the movement) steps *toward* this new, more human society.

Cult

It is unfortunate that in our day "cult" has acquired such negative connotation. Maurin's use of the word reflects its Latin root, *cultus*: that body of ritual, symbol and action through which a believing community expresses and lives out its creed and by which "ordinary" life is taken up into the sacred. It can be something as simple as making the sign of the cross before a meal or something as elaborate as a Solemn Pontifical Mass. Cultus is the outward form of inner conviction; it is devotion expressed (and nurtured) physically. Thus, when he insisted that authentic human community required common cult, Maurin meant that such community must be grounded in an enacted sense of the imminent presence of God, a God who is always "at hand" in every action of our lives — labor, reflection, play, rest.

For Maurin, it went without saying that such common cult would be Catholic and that its central rite would be the Eucharist. Yet he presumed that the web of sacramentality that finds its heart in bread and wine transformed and shared as the life-giving Body and Blood of Christ would spread throughout the whole fabric of life to grace all its aspects and activities, the greatest to the least. Maurin's model for such cult-based community was the French peasant culture of his own childhood, where the external actions of faith were a natural part of the rhythms of daily living. These actions, both personal and corporate, large and small, consciously celebrated the intimate presence of God in God's world and in every aspect of human experience.

In our own culture, so strongly molded by the Protestant rejection of traditional Christian cultus, and even in our Protestantized, post-Vatican II Roman Catholic Church itself, such sacral actions and daily rituals — especially those of the smaller, "homier" sort — tend to be viewed with suspicion (if not outright hostility) as primitive or superstitious. Maurin, however, would reject this assessment. All those small ritual actions, he would insist, tell us at every turning of our lives that God is *here*, too!

When the priest blesses the fields in the spring, sprinkling them with holy water, it reminds us that we are not alone in our toil, that we are co-laborers with God. When, at certain hours, the pace of work ceases briefly at the sound of the Angelus bell, we are brought back to the fact that time, too, is a creature in the hands of the Creator and that our lives are ultimately lived for that eternity which is outside and "alongside" time. When a candle burns before the image of a saint in our home, it is a symbol that we go about our daily activities surrounded by that "great cloud of witnesses" who have gone before us and whose faith we share.

Cult is, then, a practical means for, as Brother Lawrence puts it, "practicing the presence of God." It reminds us that God is not limited to the "spiritual;" rather, God is present in *everything* — trembling, vibrant, alive, waiting to be recognized and celebrated. In that this cult is shared, it becomes as well a kind of glue holding community together. It is an external expression of our common life in God, and that life is both the source and the means of our ability to strive for authentic community in the first place.

Dorothy Day followed Maurin quite naturally in his estimation of the centrality of cult, since what first drew her to the Church — in her desperate days of determined unbelief as a young woman — was the rich traditional piety of her Italian Catholic neighbors in New York's East Village. Indeed, even into her old age, as the post-Vatican II American Church divested itself of most of the forms and devotions that made up that piety, Dorothy was known to express hesitation over younger Workers' predilection for informal home liturgies when Father So-and-So said a perfectly acceptable daily Mass at the nearby parish church. When it came to liturgical life, she once wrote in *The Catholic Worker*, "I am afraid I am a traditionalist."

As for the authoritative source of cult, it has already been noted that Maurin firmly believed the Roman Catholic bishops to be "the appointed leaders of mankind" and his enthusiasm for personalist freedom stopped abruptly at the door of the hierarchical, authoritarian Church which he accepted on faith as the divinely appointed agent of God's will in the world. Maurin was not out to call the laity to rebellion against the worldliness or accommodationist theologies of the institutional Church or its clergy. Rather, he looked for those places where the hierarchy spoke what he understood to be the truth, lifted up these teachings as the authentic voice of Christ in his Church, and called both laity *and* clergy to a more radical submission to that voice.

It was the same for convert Dorothy Day. Despite attempts by many over the years to make of her a spokesperson for one or another form of Catholic dissent, she considered any temptation in that direction as a particularly invidious species of spiritual pride. As she explained to psychiatrist and author Robert Coles in the course of a series of interviews in the 1970s:

> I didn't become a Catholic in order to purify the church. ... It wasn't mine by birth or even youth. I came to it at the onset of my middle years. ... I felt like a lucky guest for a while, then at home, and then I did decide to try to be as loyal as possible ... and let that loyalty, if it was achieved, be my testimony, my critique. ... I have never wanted to challenge the church, only be part of it, obey it, and in return, receive its mercy and love, the mercy and love of Jesus.

Similarly, while affirming the ultimate primacy of individual conscience, Day also understood that being a Catholic meant — as Mel Piehl notes — "accepting limits on human freedom." She said on numerous occasions that, if the Cardinal Archbishop of New York at any time told her to do so, she would immediately cease publication of *The Catholic Worker* out of obedience. It is instructive to note, however, what happened on the one occasion that this intriguing declaration was put to the test.

In March of 1951, Dorothy was called to the archdiocesan offices for a meeting with Monsignor Edward Gaffney, who most certainly spoke with the authority and knowledge of his boss, the politically conservative Francis Cardinal Spellman. The Monsignor's edict: *The Catholic Worker* must either change its name (so as to omit the word "Catholic") or stop publishing. Exactly what led the chancery to act at this point is unclear. It had, after all, suffered the paper's decidedly unpopular viewpoint for nearly twenty years, ignoring calls from many quarters for its suppression. Dorothy's first biographer, William Miller, implies the provocation may have been "Christian anarchist" jibes at institutional religion in some of Ammon Hennacy's contributions to the paper. Jim Forest, in his own biography of Day, suggests Spellman may have harbored lingering antagonism toward Dorothy and the Worker for their public criticism of his handling of a strike by the archdiocesan gravediggers three years previously. For a prelate possessed of a rigid certainty as to the need for absolute lay obedience to clerical authority (as well as a robust memory for any slight to his ecclesiastical dignity), the fact that Dorothy Day and other Catholic Workers had joined the strikers in picketing his own offices was something that well might have continued to rankle — along with the Worker's refusal to join the national hue and cry against Communists, "fellow-travelers" and other agents of the "enemy within."

Whatever its ultimate cause, the chancery's ultimatum provoked one of Dorothy Day's more calculatedly nuanced responses. Although she had shown little reticence about exercising her editorial control of the paper in the past, she now informed Gaffney that any decision about the future of *The Catholic Worker* would require consultation with her co-editors. Accordingly, a short time later she wrote a letter that managed to be at once deeply submissive in tone and flatly defiant in fact.

Insisting on her "love and respectful obedience to the church, and ... gratitude to this Archdiocese," Day wrote that, while she was personally willing to change the paper's name out of obedience, those with whom she shared editorial responsibility were not. "All feel that *The Catholic Worker* has been in existence for eighteen years ... under that name, and that this is no time to change it." As for ceasing to publish, she was equally unyielding: "This would be a grave scandal to our readers and would put into the hands of ... the enemies of the church a formidable weapon."

Perhaps to the soften the hard edge of her resistance, Day added that the paper stood ready to "receive respectfully and give practical heed and application to ... all theological or spiritual censures of theological or spiritual errors" — full well knowing that the complaints against the Worker had nothing to do with its theology, which remained resolutely orthodox. She also contritely admitted she had perhaps not exercised as much control over the paper's contents as she might have and promised to oversee editorial matters more closely. Then, going on the offensive, she noted that there was no question of the Catholic War Veterans being asked to change its name, even though — like the Worker — it was a lay organization independent of any diocesan authority. She also quoted the Vatican's

own newspaper to Monsignor Gaffney, to the effect that both the Soviet and American systems were deeply flawed (a view that somehow
never managed to make its way into any of the Cardinal's public
statements on relations between the superpowers). In closing, she offered an olive branch: *The Catholic Worker* would in the future "try
to be less dogmatic, more persuasive, less irritating, more winning."
And that was that. The archdiocese chose to drop the matter. And, in
point of fact, as Jim Forest notes, there was absolutely no editorial
change in the contents of the paper, although Day did for a time become more involved in reading and approving proposed articles.

There is no doubt that Dorothy Day was far from naive about the
brokenness of the Church. As much as she loved it, she recognized
that it is, as she wrote, at the same time both "a whore" and also "our
mother" — or, on other occasions, "the cross on which Christ is cru-
cified." While it might sometimes have been considerably easier for
her to walk away from an organization that in so many respects failed
her lofty conception of its meaning and purpose, Day chose the more
difficult road of remaining its faithful daughter, confident that the
Roman Catholic Church bore and mediated — through its sacra-
ments, its teaching, and the heroic example of its saints — that very
truth of which it so often fell short institutionally.

It is important to note that Day's costly fidelity was not directed to
some metaphysical idealization of the Body of Christ that existed only
in her own mind, nor to an "underground church," nor to any gnostic
inner circle of spiritual cognoscenti. She loved and respected the everyday, prosaic, specific reality of the Roman Church, with all its
"warts, spots and wrinkles," and she sought to conform her own understanding to its teaching. To this end, she was probably one of the
few Catholic lay people in recent memory who avidly read papal en-
cyclicals for personal edification. As she wrote in the late 1930s:

> This month I've been reading the Encyclicals of the Holy
> Father as I've gone about town on the subway and the
> elevated. They are the best kind of spiritual reading be-
> cause they are directed to us now, at the present time, for
> our present needs. ... They are all pertinent, deep and
> searching in their analysis of the present day and our
> conduct at this time.

Of particular significance to both Maurin and Day were those en-
cyclicals which spoke directly to issues of justice and a renewed so-

cial order. Of these, Leo XIII's ground-breaking *De Rerum Novarum* (1891) held special meaning. A conscious attempt to apply traditional Catholic moral teaching to the new conditions created by the Industrial Revolution, *Rerum Novarum* went far beyond any previous Church teaching in its positive affirmation of workers' right to organize, the moral imperative of a just wage (so that an ordinary worker and his family might live in at least "reasonable and frugal comfort"), and the duty of the state to ensure economic equity.

This claim by the Church to a voice in economic affairs and the conditions of employment was underscored in 1931 when Pius XI issued *Quadragesimo Anno* in commemoration of the fortieth anniversary of *Rerum Novarum*. While reasserting the incompatibility of strict socialism and Catholicism (*Rerum Novarum* had also condemned socialism), Pius' encyclical noted as well the evil consequences of unrestrained laissez-faire capitalism and bureaucratic centralization, both matters of importance to Maurin's analysis.

Since the Second World War, the Catholic Worker has drawn ongoing encouragement from the Church's increasingly prophetic stance toward the accepted verities of bourgeois Western society. Indeed, the movement could only be encouraged by developments like Paul VI's apostolic letter on social justice (issued in 1971 to mark *Rerum Novarum*'s eightieth anniversary), the judgment of the Latin American bishops assembled at Puebla that authentic Christianity presumes a "preferential option" for the poor, and the repeated exhortations by John Paul II regarding the Church's negative judgment of collectivist communism and materialist capitalism alike.

In the much changed situation of the Church in this last decade of the twentieth century, it must be acknowledged that Maurin's vision of cult presumes a unanimity of opinion, not to mention a lay acquiescence to clerical authority, which simply no longer exists, at least in the Western Church. Certainly, Maurin's vision for a community drawn together by common cult becomes complicated when the very Church which is to be the source of this unifying cultus both abandons much of its own traditional practice and appears (again, at least in the West) to move toward a pluralism directly opposed to that uniformity of belief and behavior which was a conscious goal of Catholicism prior to Vatican II.

On a deeper level, neither Maurin nor Day ever fully resolved the tension between their insistence on human freedom and their matter-of-fact acceptance of hierarchical authority in the Church. Indeed, there is little evidence Maurin was even aware such a tension existed. Presumably this is because he recognized that while no human being, in and of himself or herself, can be trusted to wield power over the moral freedom of another, the God who made and sustains all things through self-emptying love is certainly to be so trusted. Indeed, such power is God's by right. The Church, therefore — viewed by Maurin as acting in the authority of and protected from error by God's Spirit — could speak in God's name and exact obedience, without that obedience in any way compromising the necessity for independent, uncoerced personalist decision in all other circumstances of human life.

Despite the fundamental theological conservatism of the movement's founders, most Worker communities today strongly reflect the "progressive" elements in current American Catholicism, including a tendency toward genial anti-clericalism and liturgical informality. For younger Workers, the monolithic Catholic culture which Maurin assumed in his teachings on cult — the immigrant Church with its feast days and devotions, its Friday fast and Saturday confession, its ritual acts great and small — is as alien as the Christendom of late medieval Europe. Most of today's Catholic Workers grew up in a church already vastly different from the one Maurin so passionately believed to be the "hope of the nations."

Yet Maurin's emphasis on cult survives — in the centrality given to breaking bread in nearly every Catholic Worker community (even if that celebration be a house liturgy led by lay men and women), in the emphasis on prayer as a source and context for prophetic action, and in the symbols that adorn most Houses of Hospitality (icons of Dorothy Day, Cesar Chavez and Martin Luther King, Jr. now joining the older images of St. Joseph the Worker and St. Martin de Porres).

Judged by the rich tradition of cult which Maurin knew and encouraged, the Worker's present cultic life may seem spare — "cult-lite," as a waspish Worker once quipped. But, in however simplified a form, the Worker witness to what Peter Maurin understood so profoundly continues: As physical beings made to love and give praise to God, we have an innate need for the rhythms and rituals that common cult provides. Cult gives structure to everyday experience, impregnating it with sacred meaning; it provides form for the inchoate longing of our hearts to know the presence of God in the often mundane routines of our daily lives. When wedded to mutual support and common purpose, cult binds us together in that authentic community which — we are promised — is a foretaste of a deeper connection that will be ours forever in the fullness of the Kingdom of God.

Culture

"Culture," the second element of Maurin's green revolution, comprises several different but related elements: rootedness in a common tradition, a personal balance between intellectual and physical pursuits, and return to a craft-based society as a remedy for the pandemic alienation engendered by the Industrial Revolution. Perhaps nowhere else is the scope of Maurin's synthesis, or the extensive reach of his encyclopedic study, more evident that in this model for renewed culture, drawing as it does from Russian utopianism, English distributist philosophy, the aesthetic theories of the arts and crafts movement, French peasant wisdom and the monastic tradition of the Church.

The Need for Roots: One of the many ways in which Maurin's vision is profoundly conservative is in its looking *backward* for meaning and social cohesion. Reflecting on his own childhood among the French peasantry, he found there a robust sense of shared roots: people recognized that they came from a "place" (where their ancestors might have lived for literally a millennium) and that they had a "story" of a shared past which was respected and celebrated and which gave them a common understanding not only about who they were in the present, but also about what they should be in the future.

Looking around him at then-contemporary American society, Maurin saw just the opposite: with the mobility that characterized the American experience from the beginning and which was only compounded by the dislocations of the Great Depression, few Americans had a sense of place extending back more than a decade or two at most; under the theory of the melting pot, immigrants, or at least certainly their second-generation children, were anxious to divest themselves of time-honored customs and tradition as quickly as possible; in the crush of American cities isolation and fragmentation were the norm. Instead of roots and a common story, America offered the hope of wages and a Ford automobile, and to Maurin this seemed a poor exchange, leaving men and women adrift and disconnected, vulnerable not only to the despair bred of existential estrangement, but also to the seductions of materialism and consumerism rushing in to fill the void left by lack of grounded identity.

Sixty-some years later, the irony is that the America Maurin so trenchantly critiqued in the 1930s now appears a model of rootedness and commonality of values compared to the splintered, factionalized, individualistic present. Today, most Western lives are experienced as independent projects of self-creation having little reference to anything beyond the atomized ego. Today, as study after study informs us, the young are united in their ignorance of the past and in a conviction that "history" (which seems to include all events preceding the date of one's own birth) is a bore — unless it can be recycled and merchandized as "retro" fashion.

This is not to say that all appreciation of our hunger for a connection with some common heritage has been utterly abandoned. Rather, and perhaps worse, tradition has been wrenched from the collective consciousness and made simply one more commodity to be packaged and sold, whether through the up-market counsels of gracious living maven Martha Stewart or in the nostalgic visual references to a highly-fictionalized past which regularly appear as props in television commercials for everything from automobiles to packaged breakfast food.

In the light of such a present, even more than was the case in his own day, Maurin's insistence on what French Christian humanist Simone Weil would later term "the need for roots" represents not only a radical departure from but, the Worker would argue, a desperately needed antidote to the splintering and confusion which mark so much of contemporary life. In looking backward, rootedness grounds us in more than ourselves. It reminds us that our individual stories are part of a larger narrative, and it provides a stable context for the unique psycho-spiritual journey to which each of us is called by virtue of our birth into the human family.

The Meaning of Labor: Maurin perceived that men and women after the Industrial Revolution were not only cut off from their roots; they were also divided in the wholeness of their own beings through the severing of intellectual activity from physical labor. The fortunate and the educated worked with their minds, if they worked at all, and were generally paid relatively well. If not part of the plutocracy or the professions, they were at least "white-collar" workers. Members of the minimally educated "blue-collar" underclass, on the other hand, spent their lives at manual labor and earned far less, because — however necessary their work might be — it was seen as intrinsically less valuable because it was physical.

While from the beginning of the Industrial Revolution a number of reform movements had attempted by various means to meet the educational, cultural, social and even sporting needs of the working class, the "bosses" in general were not entirely comfortable with a worker who thought too much — it made him a potential nuisance, too readily open to subversive ideas. It was also widely held that the lower classes didn't really require much of an intellectual or aesthetic life anyway, since they lacked the innate sensibility necessary for true culture.

Conversely, the businessman, professional, academic or artist was hardly expected to "waste" time performing tasks that could be done by any "common laborer" (other than the hobbyist's puttering about in the garden on weekends) and for an educated person to be "reduced" to subsisting by the work of his hands and back would be a truly shameful fall in status. In short, mental work was prized, physical work devalued, and this fact was evidenced in class structures, social conventions, educational policy, and the hard reality of cash compensation.

To be fair, such attitudes were hardly the creation *ex nihilo* of the Industrial Revolution or mercantile capitalism. Nearly every society in recorded history has enfleshed the principle of the leisure class. In more than one, the ability to avoid any gainful employment by living off the toil of others has been viewed as a mark of superior quality, a notion which perhaps reached its apotheosis in the English concept of the "gentleman" so memorably depicted in the novels of Jane Austin. Further, since Maurin's day, with the unionization of industrial labor and, more recently, the rise of a "service economy," traditional white collar/blue collar categories have become to some extent passé. Unionized assembly-line workers have through collective bargaining gained income levels which put them well into the middle class, while many clerical workers who perform no physical labor nevertheless remain near the bottom of the wage scale. Despite this, the basic cultural divide between those who earn their living with their brains and those who earn it with their bodies remains, as does humankind's perennial contempt for manual labor.

As Maurin saw it, this contempt is based upon a misunderstanding of the significance of physical work. While it is true that Dorothy Day once wrote that "Labor is a discipline imposed on all of us because of the fall," in Maurin's view, work is not a curse, despite the words of God in Genesis as Adam and Eve are driven out of Paradise: "cursed is the ground because of you; through the sweat of your brow will you eat of it all the days of your life." Although there is no evidence he ever did so, Maurin would have been justified in noting that, even before the expulsion, the primal couple were set to tending God's garden oasis as stewards of the created bounty. ("The Lord God took the man and put him in the garden of Eden to till it and keep it.") What changed outside Eden's gates was not that humankind suddenly had to work for the first time, but that its work would forever after be thwarted by an often resistant and unresponsive nature. In the mythic imagery of Genesis, the rupture of the natural symbiosis between creator and human by the catastrophe of sin is mirrored in a breach of the intended cooperation between humans and the rest of creation over which they have been placed as God's vicars. But this breach does not lessen the dignity of human labor, it merely places that labor in a new and more difficult context.

In fact, far from being a curse, physical labor, Maurin declared, is a *gift* of creation. Work, effort, sweat — these are good, necessary things. Our bodies are made for them, and without them those bodies sicken and bloat. In this belief, Maurin reflected the Russian anarchist Kropotkin, who wrote:

> Work, labor, is a physiological necessity, a necessity of spending accumulated bodily energy, a necessity which is health and life itself.

Further, Maurin argued, physical work is the primary medium through which we cooperate with God in nurturing the gifts of the earth and transforming those gifts into food and objects of usefulness and beauty. This process of human labor cooperating with God in the divine action of creation is a fundamental part of what it means to be a human being.

And not only is the gift of labor a good thing, it is a *holy* thing. Our spirits require it to be healthy and complete. "To work," as Augustine put it, "is to pray." Echoing the saint, Maurin taught: "Labor ought to be a prayer." In physical work, conscientiously and gratefully performed, the human person fulfills an integral aspect of his or her humanness, and thereby — in living out the Creator's intent — gives glory to God.

Thus, Maurin taught, both the "gentleman" and the proletarian are wounded in their essential humanity by the notion that physical work is something demeaning rather than an ennobling and indispensable element of God's purpose in our creation. In work, we use our bodies to do what is healthy for us physically and spiritually, we fulfill our God-given role as co-creators, and we make appropriate use of the gifts of creation, for its benefit as well as our own. Thus, by our labor, our own vitality is served, God's glory is made manifest and nature's bounty is enhanced and increased for the common good. Comparing the balance and beauty of this intended design to our contemporary emphasis on "fitness," one can hardly miss a poignant irony: Those whose employment is sedentary, and therefore more respected and better paid, expend large amounts of money and effort in gyms and health clubs working up the sweat from which their affluence frees them — and yet produce nothing in the process but more shapely temples to their own well-being.

Maurin took the consequences of human labor's significance even further: If our work is a holy gift and a means of our participation as co-creators with God in the outworking of creation, then:

> Labor is not a commodity
> to be bought and sold.
> Labor is a means of self-expression,
> the worker's gift to the Common Good.

This conviction led Maurin to what is arguably the most radical aspect of his teaching, a call to reject the controlling power of "wage slavery" by breaking the connection between labor and compensation through a personal decision to treat one's labor in an entirely new way:

> But they say
> that there is no work to do.
> There is plenty of work to do,
> but no wages.
> But people do not need to work for wages,
> they can offer their services as a gift.

Personalist that he was, Maurin saw no need to wait around until the prevailing system changed. If working for a wage demeaned and disfigured the worker's relationship to his or her labor, then workers should "fire the bosses." In other words (to borrow a phrase from the 1960s), they should "drop-out" of the whole capitalist wage system — not in favor of sloth or non-productive dependency, but to the end that they might put their energy and skills to use for those purposes for which they are intended, self-sufficiency and the good of the community. In Maurin's view, one can choose to do what needs to be done for the common good and not worry about remuneration, trusting that God will supply one's needs (if one is content to live simply). Lest his counsel seem utterly quixotic, Maurin admitted that such an approach might be difficult to sustain in an urban environment. But that was just one more thing that was wrong with the urban environment and one more reason that urban industrial workers should go "back to the land," where, in cooperative self-sufficiency, there would be "no unemployment," even in a depression.

If such a proposal sounded extreme, that did not concern Maurin. His purpose was "not to help people to adjust themselves to the existing environment;" it was to challenge them to begin living by the truth of their creation. That challenge brooked no compromise or half-steps:

The best means
are the pure means,
and the pure means
are the heroic means.

It was this "heroic" absolutism regarding work — along with his insistence that cooperation, not confrontation, is the only effective strategy for positive social change — which led to Maurin's rejection of organized labor and its methods as a solution for industrial workers' ills. As far as Maurin was concerned, the unions (especially the Gompers-style "pocketbook" unionism which had supplanted the labor movement's earlier radicalism) were no different from entrepreneurial capitalism in their understanding of the meaning of work. Both treated the worker's toil as something to which a price (albeit, in the case of the unions, a higher price) could be affixed, rather than treating it as a sacred gift. Therefore the unions, as much as the "bosses," participated in the "commercialization" of labor, which to Maurin was nothing less than a sacrilege.

As already noted, Dorothy Day disagreed and it was her view that prevailed in the Worker. She accepted, at least in theory, Maurin's principles regarding the ultimate goal of "work not wages" (a slogan which particularly moved her when she saw it on a placard at a labor demonstration). In the short term, however, she believed workers deserved as much economic justice as organization, collective bargaining and labor action (including the strike) could obtain for them. Since Christians are called to work for justice, then — she argued —

Christians should support the legitimate efforts of workers attempting to better their lot, however imperfectly. As a result, Day and the Workers offered not only "propaganda" support for various labor actions in the pages of *The Catholic Worker* and other Worker communities' publications, but practical support as well, providing food and shelter to strikers, picketing with them and (as with Dorothy Day's last arrest with the United Farm Workers in 1973) going to jail with them.

Yet despite its deviation from Maurin's views on organized labor, the Worker has continued to uphold his vision that work is most perfectly what it is intended by God to be when given freely and faithfully for the common good. If one is tempted to dismiss this element of Maurin's thought as hopelessly unrealistic it may be helpful to remember that it is precisely this that members of the Worker movement have been doing for over sixty years. Seeing that the poor need to be fed, sheltered, comforted, Catholic Workers have used the time the rest of us take up with "gainful employment" doing just those things, in many cases working much harder than the typical wage-earner in exchange for nothing more than voluntary poverty — a basic sufficiency for which they beg and which they share with the poor.

Reason and Creativity Are Gifts to All: While upholding the sanctity and necessity of labor, Maurin also recognized that the human person requires more than physical work to be complete and fulfilled — every person is intended by God to have an intellectual and aesthetic life as well. There are differences in individual talent and aptitude, to be sure, but reason and creativity are our common birthright, bestowed so that we may more wholly respond to the love of God, more fully enjoy the gifts of creation, and more significantly enrich those gifts by our participation in the human story.

To Maurin, there was a kind of blasphemy in the widespread blunting of laboring lives by repetitive, mindless and often meaningless work, by inferior schooling and by the pervasive mediocrity of the mass media. This dulling of potential was a spiritual issue because it defaced the image of God in its victims. The grinding poverty of those at the very bottom of the capitalist heap — the unemployed urban poor, the homeless, migrant laborers and sharecroppers — was even more destructive to humans' inborn need to think about, delight in, and more deeply understand themselves, their world and the God who made both.

In the face of a generalized, and not always benign, condescension toward the capacities of the masses, Maurin insisted that — just as much as the educated and privileged — the poor and the workers have eyes, ears, minds, and imaginations that need to be kindled and stimulated so that they might fully live out the purpose of their creation. Such intellectual and aesthetic development is as much a part of God's passionate desire for their wholeness as is economic justice or moral and spiritual renewal. Thus, it is not only labor that is sacred. Informed thought and creative expression are also holy. In developing our minds and putting to use our imaginative abilities, we give enacted praise to the God who is the source of those gifts and who delights in our exercise of them.

It is this conviction which has assured a place in the movement for graphic artists such as Ade Bethune, who adopted Maurin's suggestion that Christ and the saints be portrayed as workers, and Quaker Fritz Eichenberg, whose striking woodcuts have been a notable feature of *The Catholic Worker* since they first began appearing in its pages in 1950 and whose "Christ of the Breadlines" may well be the single graphic image most associated with the Worker movement.

Creation versus Consumption: Maurin appears to have been more concerned with fostering an intellectual life for workers and the poor than he was with developing their aesthetic appreciation — at any rate, he certainly lacked Dorothy Day's passionate, lifelong appreciation of music and literature. Nonetheless, his emphasis on the importance of liberating and nurturing the capacities of each human mind speaks profoundly to our own day, in which nearly every form of creative expression and recreation has been professionalized, with the result that even well educated people experience life almost exclusively as consumers of other people's creativity.

Seventy years ago, for example, especially in smaller communities, the need of the human spirit to express itself in music was met not only by various amateur orchestras and chorales but also by the institution of the "community sing," in which neighbors gathered simply to make music. The point was not the caliber of performance but the joy of singing itself, with the added benefit of bringing people together. Today, with television, radio, tapes and CDs, the ascendancy of the professional performer is nearly complete: Now when we think of music we have in mind something we listen to, not something we ourselves make.

Similarly, the storytelling that is so central and unifying a factor in more traditional societies has given way in our own day to the domination of mass market myth-makers: the creators of television and film. Most of us do not recount the formative legends of the community to our children — we sit them down with a video and let Hollywood spoon-feed them the icons by which their burgeoning imaginations will be developed (or, more often, narrowed). In both these instances, and many more like them, a gift given by God for our pleasure in its expression has been transformed into a commodity which we purchase and ingest; something God provided as ours to *do* has become something that is someone else's to *sell*. Creation yields to consumption, action to passive reception.

This is not to say that there is no place for the uniquely gifted professional artist, creator or performer. What is foreign to Maurin's vision is the notion of the artist as ultimate individualist (and social rebel), answerable to nothing and no one but his or her own genius, as well as the consequent scorn for the "amateur" that follows upon such elevation of the artist into a species apart from the rest of us.

For Maurin, creativity and talent, like all other gifts, are given for the common good and the glory of God, and the artist — like every other child of God — is intended to be grounded in a community. He may sometimes express the community's vision, she may sometimes challenge that vision, but always the artist must speak *out of, for* and *to* the community.

There is no place in Maurin's vision for either the patronage system of the Renaissance in which enjoyment and possession of art is a privilege restricted to the wealthy, or the commercialization of art that marks bourgeois society after the Industrial Revolution, in which the artist's creation becomes simply one more product to be merchandized and purchased (often more as a sign of status than of genuine aesthetic response). On the other hand, Maurin's perspective also offers scant comfort to the Romantic view that the artist is called only to "express" his or her own vision and, should the community not understand that vision, that's the community's problem.

Rather, when Maurin spoke of art and artists, he repeatedly turned back to the Middle Ages, often holding up the model of the cathedral of Chartres, a continuing glory which resulted from the collaborative efforts of countless anonymous artists and artisans who over generations offered their skills to honor God and to provide their community with a focus for the cultus which bound it together. For Maurin, creativity and talent, like every other gift of our creation, are best used when they flow from love of God and a generous embrace of one's partners in community, thereby producing the good (which may sometimes be difficult), the true (which may sometimes be obnoxious), and the beautiful (which will always be enlivening).

The Worker-Scholar: As Maurin saw it, then, in order to restore the intended wholeness of human life, the affluent needed to embrace physical labor and proletarians needed to be freed and empowered to claim their intellectual and creative birthright. Until this happened, the culturally sanctioned rift between physical work and reflection would ensure that everyone continued to live truncated, incomplete lives.

Maurin's often-repeated answer to this rift was the model of the "worker-scholar," a model he drew from the Rule of St. Benedict, under which life was arranged to incorporate a daily balance between physical labor, prayer and study. Such a life, Maurin insisted, was not just a matter of condescending justice (the scholar deigning to do his or her "share" of the work). Without labor, the scholar became less fully human; without study and reflection, the worker too was diminished; and, without prayer, both were cut off from the ultimate source of meaning for their physical work and their mental and creative activities as well.

The worker-scholar, on the other hand, while developing and making use of his or her particular gifts or talents, would nevertheless be a whole person rather than a "specialist." She would have time each day to put to use the muscles and dexterity with which God gifted her, to fully inhabit her physical body. He would have freedom to think, learn, and create — not just for a few years devoted to study in youth, before "real" work began, but each day throughout his life. Labor and craft, mental and creative activity — all would be balanced in a context of obedient intentionality created by daily prayer. In that context, both physical and intellectual effort would be directed toward ends that were right, fruitful and just — in short, in accord with the loving purpose of God.

How are scholars to become workers and workers scholars? By crossing over the barriers of class and custom that bourgeois society places between them and living and working together, fulfilling the spiritual work of mercy of "instructing the ignorant" by teaching each other what they know. Arthur Sheehan, in his biography, expressed Maurin's teaching on this point eloquently:

In working side by side with the worker, the scholar
would be using his hands as well as his head and would
learn what matter had to tell him, while the worker would
be learning what the spirit had to say. ... Out of this
synthesis of matter and spirit would come art. Men would
find the beauty they craved, for which they starved in a
wasteland of industrialism.

In a sense, the vision of the worker-scholar is the very core of
Maurin's anthropology. The worker-scholar is what God intended for
us in our creation. Only in the symmetry of such a life can we begin
to live out the fullness of God's purpose for us. Yet, Maurin saw
clearly, so long as workers continued to live under the conditions imposed on them by industrial capitalism, they would lack the time, energy and opportunity for the pursuits of the scholar. Personal choice
alone would not be enough to liberate most workers to develop their
intellectual and creative gifts — not only would individual hearts have
to change, the structure of society itself would have to be altered. To
this end, what Maurin called for was nothing less than a complete
rejection of the deformed culture created by the Industrial Revolution
and its replacement by an older, more human form of social organization.

Rejecting the Industrial Revolution: Viewing the Industrial Revolution and its aftermath as nothing less than an unmitigated spiritual
catastrophe, Maurin saw no need for accommodation or compromise.
Rather, he proposed a truly radical alternative: a voluntary return to a
village, craft-based society in which the right relationship between
worker and work could be restored and political relationships would
remain human-scaled — clearly an impossibility in the massiveness of
the industrialized city. This turning back to a pre-industrial social
model, Maurin insisted, was not a utopian ideal to be effected only at
some future, more propitious moment in history; it was a choice to be
embraced, worked for and moved toward *now*, in the spirit of the personalist mandate to take responsibility upon oneself and act in accord
with what is real, apart from any antecedent change in larger social
structures and systems.

Always the synthesizer, Maurin drew from a number of related
sources to create his vision of what such an alternative community
would be like. All of them had in common a rejection of industrializa-

tion and its consequences — urbanization, the standardization of product, the factory (later, the assembly-line), and loss by workers of the means of production and distribution. From Marxist analysis (and his own experience as a "common laborer") came Maurin's searing critique of the alienation bred by industrial capitalism. In the utopian writings of Tolstoy and the essays of the anarchist Prince Kropotkin he found paradigms for village communalism that would transcend previous class-stratified models.

English "distributist" thinkers G. K. Chesterton, Father Vincent McNabb and Hilaire Belloc provided much of the theoretical basis for Maurin's condemnation of industrial urbanization and his call for a return to earlier forms of social organization. Sometimes scorned by critics for their alleged "romanticism," the distributists, along with a number of other quasi-reactionary English groups in the 1930s, were anti-capitalist, anti-industrialist, anti-urban and anti-statist. As did Maurin, they advocated decentralization, a recovery of the spiritual nature of work, and repudiation of the oppressively large, impersonal structures of industrial society in favor of smaller, more interactive social arrangements. Along with the distributists, the earlier but related English arts and crafts movement, exemplified by utopian socialist William Morris, offered a vision for restoring individual artistry and genuine craft to every worker's labor, and this movement had a significant influence on Worker thought through the writing and example of Catholic artist and communitarian Eric Gill. Maurin was clearly speaking out of this distributist, arts and crafts tradition when he boldly asserted:

> Creative labor is craft labor. Mechanized labor is not creative labor. Workmen cannot find happiness in mechanized work.

From the very beginning of the Industrial Revolution, there had been reaction and resistance — sometimes violent — to the wrenching changes industrialization brought in its wake. In England, the early 1800s saw displaced handworkers known as Luddites (after a possibly legendary Leicestershire workingman named Ned Ludd) attacking the mills and smashing the new mass-production machinery that had rendered them redundant and unemployed. Later, tenant farmers drove off survey teams for the railroads by force, convinced that this new transportation marvel would not only cause their livestock to abort but (more astutely) that it would destroy the character of rural English life.

From our own perspective nearly two hundred years later, with the triumph of industrialization a given (and indeed made somewhat passé by the subsequent technological revolution), it can be hard to understand what all the fuss was about. Many of us may from time to time regret the monotony or ultimate meaninglessness of the work we do; we may upon occasion complain of the stresses of urban life or the distractions and seductions of our culture of consumption, but more often than not we accept not only the inevitability but, at least in general terms, the positive value of the world as we find it — it is, after all, the result of "progress."

To begin to understand what Maurin saw (and what the Worker continues to see) as the fatal flaws in industrialization, a homely (and admittedly simplified) example may be useful:

Consider a chair. In a pre-industrial society, that chair is typically produced by one craftsperson who does the entire job from start to finish, using his or her own tools. When the chair is completed it is the possession of the one who made it; it may be used, sold or given away as he or she sees fit. Being the product of such a process, this chair is unique — no other, even from the hand of the same creator, can ever be exactly like it.

In an industrial society, the situation is quite different. The chair is produced in a factory; a particular worker does one or more of the steps involved in making such chairs over and over again day after day, never seeing the entire process through from start to finish. The factory owner has possession of the "tools" — now, in actuality, machines — by which the chair is made and when the chair is completed he owns it as well, paying a wage to the worker for his or her labor. Being the product of this process, such a chair is far from unique — hundreds, even thousands of identical chairs may be manufactured by this and other factories using the same machinery and specifications.

"Well, what," the factory owner might ask, "is wrong with any of that? Jobs are created, product is provided to meet the demands of the mass market, and quality (by means of uniformity) is assured." And it must be admitted that the industrial model is the vastly more *efficient* of the two: Many more chairs are made in far less time and at far less cost. But, the distributists and Maurin with them cautioned, in pursuit of all that efficiency, something of vital significance has happened to both worker and factory owner.

The worker no longer participates in the entire operation and has little or no control over even his or her own small portion of it. Having no part in decisions about what will be made, or how it will be made, the worker merely performs that portion of the task assigned, thereby losing any personal stake in the end result and, with it, the creative satisfaction and pride of workmanship that accompany involvement in the full process from beginning to end. In short, the worker has ceased to be a creator and become merely a cog in the larger production machine. Further, since workers no longer possess the means of production, they of necessity work at the discretion of the owner, especially in the absence of organized labor. Thus, the owner not only controls the process and the tools utilized for that process but also, in a very real sense, "owns" the workers themselves, as they have sold their labor for a wage — hence the term "wage slave."

This rending of workers from the wholeness and meaning of their work and their consequent dependency on an employer and a paycheck are what Marx diagnosed so accurately as the "alienation" created by industrial capitalism. For Maurin, that alienation was a profoundly *spiritual* issue, spiritual because — if the theological assumption that we are intended by God to be co-creators is true — the industrial model violates the divine intent for the human person by denying workers their dignity as co-creators and destroying any real possibility of their experiencing the sacredness of their own labor.

And, though it might surprise us, the owner or "boss" also suffers in the industrial model. To be sure, he stands to make out well financially, presuming his business is a success, but however much he (or, in the rare instance, she) may control the direction of the process, he has no authentic, hands-on participation in it. Therefore, he too — fortunate as he may seem by society's standards — is impoverished spiritually by being less than the co-creator he was intended to be; he, too, is alienated from the holiness of work.

There is a further problem as well: In the industrial (and post-industrial) model, just as the ultimate point is not the wholeness or creativity of the process of production, it is not even, finally, the integrity of the product itself — whether it is good, useful or beautiful. The focus is making, as cheaply as possible, something that can be *sold*. The sale, or "point of purchase," is the *raison d'être* of the entire enterprise, not the thing produced.

The product itself can be shoddy, worthless, ugly, or dangerous; the process by which it is made destructive to human dignity, human health or the environment — none of that matters so long as it sells. If it sells, it is a success — and the entrepreneurial class which thrives on that success will prosper. But to Maurin, as to the distributists, the industrial system that creates such "success" is nothing less than demonic — a war waged upon reality which results in alienation (for both worker and employer), in aesthetic and spiritual shoddiness and in blighting of the good gifts of creation.

It might be objected, late in this century, that such a diabolical picture of industrialization and its consequences, even if to some extent justified by the first one hundred and twenty-five years of the Industrial Revolution, has long since been rendered historically obsolete by the ascendancy of the trade unions and the extensive labor and environmental legislation put into effect in the Western democracies since the Great Depression. Setting aside the ongoing erosion of such governmental interventionism over the last decade, the co-opting of the major unions by an increasingly corporate mentality, and the reality that many (if not most) of the goods we use every day are produced in countries lacking both effective unions and any legal protections for their workers, the fact remains that such adjustments to the fundamental employer/employee relationship in industrial capitalism, whether encoded in law or obtained through collective bargaining agreements, do no more than ameliorate certain of the effects of industrialization. They do not address the fundamental spiritual violence industrial development, by its very nature, does to the human person. They may, so long as they remain, provide relief to some of industrialization's symptoms, but at the cost of legitimizing the disease itself.

A more cogent criticism of distributist analysis might be that craftsmanship is labor and time intensive and, as a result, its products are prohibitively costly for all but the very rich. Former Catholic Worker John Cort made just this point many years ago after Eric Gill was imprudent enough to send *The Catholic Worker* a *type-written* denunciation of mechanization: "If industrialism as we have known it stinks, how are you going to produce typewriters cheap enough so more than a few men like yourself can buy them?" Further, it certainly could be argued that distributist models of craft versus mass production have become anachronistic in this present post-industrial, technological age: It's all well and good to speak of one artisan making a chair, but when it comes to computer chips, a Boeing 757 aircraft or a VCR, the paradigm quickly becomes ludicrous. Who would claim that a "better" computer would result from individual "computer craftsmen" toiling in isolation to build each hard-drive and screen from start to finish? The very qualities the distributists so disdained in mass-produced commodities (uniformity and standardization, in particular) are, in fact, absolutely essential to the highly technical products of the Information Age.

It is dangerous to attempt to speak for the dead, but the question must be faced as to how Maurin or the distributists whose work he incorporated into his own vision would respond to this brave new technological world we now inhabit. Are their views nothing more than a curious reactionary footnote to the inevitable and fruitful march of progress and technology — the first poignant case of "future shock?" Is the Worker foolish when it continues to uphold and promote distributist ideals in the face of the approaching third millennium?

As for Maurin, it's hard not to suspect that he would cast a decidedly jaundiced eye on many of the most prized achievements of Western technocracy and quickly return the argument to fundamental issues: Is the ability to "surf" the Internet in the comfort of one's living room worth the loss of the fullness of intended human identity? Are the technological feats of this generation, impressive though they be, a reasonable trade for the groundlessness, materialism and institutionalized violence of our current culture? No matter how delightful and even apparently useful our creations, can they heal the fundamental wounding being done to our souls and our world?

"Fast Food" and the Hunger for Community: One need not look far to find a compelling example of just how pervasive that wounding can be.

"Fast food" is a major American industry and an ubiquitous part of life for almost every person in this country. Yet the product itself is generally unhealthy, riddled with the saturated fat and salt that are major contributors to the average American's tendency to obesity and coronary disease and "enhanced" with various chemical additives of dubious or unknown effect on long-term human well-being. Fast food "culture" is also destructive to family life, as it further splinters the generations and obliterates the spiritual significance of family as community, breaking bread together around the common table. Nationwide (now worldwide) franchising inevitably represses regional and ethnic diversity (part of what is unique and irreplaceable about each of us), as every franchise serves up exactly the same fare, often driving out of business in the process less lucrative sole proprietorships which more fully reflect regional traditions.

At the same time, the generally young or otherwise marginalized workers in fast food outlets are poorly paid (the infamous "McJob" that is the first work experience for so many young people), and the work itself is rote and meaningless — operating food preparation machines rather than learning the art that cooking can be.

And not only our own society is injured; as more and more beef is required for all those hamburgers ("So Many Billion Sold!" the signs proudly proclaim), thousands of acres of irreplaceable rain forest in South America — where land is cheap — are destroyed and given over to cattle ranching, with deleterious effect not only on the global environment but on indigenous populations displaced and turned from self-sufficiency (at however modest a level) to employment by these new outposts of multinational capitalism.

There is a final, obscene cap to this ziggurat of profit and despoliation: the advertising that keeps the whole enterprise in motion. In a bitter irony, this advertising has as one of its recurring themes an appeal to our hunger for the very thing that fast food destroys: the sharing of a meal as a medium of human connection. The models in television advertisements — carefully chosen for their diversity and bathed in honeyed light — pass through the doors of their idealized fast food restaurant as into a shrine: Single parents pause in their busy day to smile with their children; elderly men and women find romance over the salad bar; teenagers grin beneath paper hats, utterly fulfilled by the prospect of serving up one more order of McNuggets and fries for minimum wage; friends are made, community is born. The not so subliminal message? The solution to our painful isolation and estrangement can be found in a "Happy Meal."

Consumption as a Substitute for Meaning: The fast food industry is hardly alone in its claims that our existential longings can be assuaged through consumption of its products. Such exploitation of our spiritual poverty is a primary tool of *all* the advertising that plays so significant a role in our current culture, advertising that Dorothy Day once perceptively denounced as "only increas[ing] people's useless desires."

Day saw clearly that, once we lose the essential connection with meaningful work which can fulfill our inborn need to be co-creators in God's world, we are left with a hunger that must be satisfied in some other way. The capitalist system, with diabolic genius, is quick to provide such a substitute for authentic fulfillment: If we are not to be creators, we can become consumers. Our longing for significance will be answered by *things*.

Unfortunately for the system, however, there is a natural limit to most people's appetite for possessions — satiation must eventually set in. It is at this juncture that advertising becomes vitally important, as it concocts new desires we never knew we had until advertising created them.

Worse, advertising does not even deal honestly with us in manufacturing these freshly minted, ersatz "needs." Rather, it calculatedly plays on our sexual drives, our fears of inadequacy, our aspirations to image and status, our anxiety about being included, and then — having roused these deep and often spiritually destructive cravings — offers things that cannot, in themselves, even remotely satisfy them. From the "always a bridesmaid never a bride" ads for mouthwash of a previous generation, to the bikini-clad "spokesmodel" at the auto show, to the artfully created sham emotionalism of the latest long distance telephone company campaign, advertising has been and continues to be a titillating game of bait and switch — stirring up thirsts it cannot quench, promising gratification when the best it can offer is temporary distraction.

While it is a truth common to all the great religious traditions that happiness is found in what sort of people we become, not in what things we acquire, the advertising that fuels our economy continues to divert us from our true spiritual needs by its calculated, shrill insistence that — in the next purchase — we will finally find the peace of soul that only authentic living can truly provide. In so doing, it provides the carrot that keeps the worker at his or her machine, desk or shop counter: Meaningless labor is necessary to earn the money to buy the things the system spews out to blind us to the fact that what we really long for is real, useful, creative work. Given all this, it is little wonder that Dorothy Day reserved some of her most stinging rebukes for advertisers ("woe to that generation") and insisted that one committed to Christ's command of love, and therefore to the common good, would of necessity be excluded from participation in such employment.

The Distributist Alternative — A Return to Village & Craft: Despite their uncompromising critique of the spiritual consequences of industrialization and consumer capitalism, Maurin, Day and the Workers after them proposed more than jeremiads and condemnation, justified as both might be. The distributist alternative society contemplated by Maurin is an ambitious (and admittedly difficult to achieve) model for a truly integrated life which would make it possible for men and women to begin to fulfill the high calling of their creation: to be worker-scholars and co-creators whose labor counts for something in the ongoing gift of human history.

And what would such an alternative look like? It would be to some extent (varying according to circumstances and the decisions of those involved) communal, living out through its external organization the spiritual interconnectedness and mutual responsibility of all its members. Its economics would involve voluntary sharing of resources on the Marxist and early Christian principle of "from each according to his or her ability, to each according to his or her need."

Maurin did not prescribe the absolute abolition of private property, however. "I am not opposed to private property with responsibility," he said, "But those who own private property should never forget that it is a trust ... not an absolute right ... [it is] a gift which . . . must be administered for the benefit of God's children." Similarly, Dorothy Day often approvingly quoted Eric Gill's aphorism, "Property is proper to man." At the same time, she was quick to acknowledge the truth of St. Gertrude's observation regarding property: [T]he more common, the more holy it is."

In one of his relatively rare attempts at practical specificity, Maurin suggested that each family in the commune have its own modest cottage and individual garden, but that the private parcels be small in comparison to the acreage farmed communally. This was not, for Maurin, simply a matter of distributive justice. Work is more satisfying as a group activity, he taught, so working together on the common land would be more enjoyable — and it would allow for *discussion* while working, thereby uniting manual labor and intellectual stimulation in one activity!

Ultimately, insofar as the question of private property was concerned, what mattered for both Maurin and Day was love in action, not abstract theoretical orthodoxy. Family members share what is theirs without thought of staking individual claim. Just so, the sort of community Maurin envisioned would understand itself to be in a familial relationship — referring to each other and to the poor as "brother" and "sister" would be more than pious (or radical) rhetoric, it would be an acknowledgment of fact. Such a community, Maurin believed, grounded in the self-emptying love of God, would share what it had spontaneously — where there was need, there would lie right to use — and so the aim of common possession would be achieved without the doctrinaire imposition of a principle.

Most Catholic Workers over the years have agreed that such a community should be no larger than a village, small enough so that all its members could meaningfully participate in making the choices affecting their life together. (In fact, in the 1960s, *The Catholic Worker* was one of the first American publications to feature the "small is beautiful" writings of E. F. Schumacher.) On the point of size, however, if Sheehan's biography of Maurin is to be trusted, Peter had a somewhat different perspective. According to Sheehan, Maurin thought the population of the commune was relatively unimportant so long as it contained a good balance between farmers and craftsmen (and presumably — although Sheehan doesn't mention it — scholars). "Even a thousand families might not be too many," Sheehan quotes Maurin as saying. Since Maurin's own family of origin included over twenty children, it would appear his vision was expansive enough to accommodate a commune of upwards of ten thousand members, proportions difficult to reconcile with the distributist call for human-scaled decentralization. But when Maurin was in his enthusiastic mode, his penchant for hyperbole could bring him close to (and occasionally beyond) boosterism, and it is perhaps in this light that his comment is best understood.

Whatever the community's size, the ultimate measure of any decision made or action taken would be the common good rather than individual advantage, that good being understood in the framework of a united commitment to a common cult. Shared effort would be exerted toward shared goals reflecting shared values. When conflicts as to the specific application of these values arose, they would be resolved through patience, self-emptying love and mutual toleration.

Unlike the typical pre-industrial village, however, this community would be classless — there would be no "lord of the manor," no dependent tenancy of the disenfranchised. Rather, all would stand on equal footing; leadership, if required, would be by invitation and example rather than the imposition of authority. The community envisioned by Maurin would also differ from many previous attempts at utopian communalism in that membership would be inclusive rather than limited through selection by affinity, whether of conviction or temperament. The poor, the outcast, the difficult and the incapacitated would be welcomed in the name of Christ and treated as equals with unique and necessary gifts to share, even if such gifts consisted only of their need. They too would be part of the family that such community must become and the concept of family would extend, finally, as far as the reach of the love of God itself.

In this cooperativist community there would be a return to the craftsman model of production: One worker (or a small collective) would build what was needed from start to finish, maintaining the integrity and creativity of the process. Tools would be owned by those workers using them, or held in common by the community on their behalf, and such distribution as there was would likewise remain under the control of the workers. The things made would be useful, beautiful and necessary. The limitless superfluity of product that marks consumer capitalism would be, of necessity, replaced by simplicity. Self-sufficiency would be the goal. Dorothy Day was later to write, in this spirit, that the community should limit its consumption to those foods produced in its own region, accepting the inevitable monotony of such a diet as one more aspect of voluntary poverty — though the Worker continued serving coffee to its guests! Nonetheless, Maurin seemed ready to adjust principle to a limited degree and allow utilization of at least some of the mass-produced products from "outside." (When a tractor was introduced at the first Catholic Worker farm at Easton, however, one person reportedly quipped, "Don't let Peter hear about this!")

For the members of such a commune, there would be an intentional ordering of daily life so that each person participated in regular, productive physical labor and each also had time for intellectual and creative pursuits. Expression in every form of art and craft would be a shared gift for enriching the whole community, not a commodity to be possessed and enjoyed by only the privileged few. While making room for unique individual talents, the emphasis in all forms of the arts would be on active participation rather than passive observation and consumption.

Through the rhythms and rituals of a common cult, men's and women's eyes would be opened to see the sacredness that floods all of creation. The "holy, holy, holy" of the angels around God's throne — recounted in both the vision of Isaiah in the Hebrew Scriptures and the Revelation to St. John at the close of the New Testament — would resonate not only in the *Sanctus* of the mass, but in all the actions of daily life, however mundane.

In sum total, then, Maurin's vision was a social construct in which men and women would — even in a broken world — be afforded opportunity to know themselves, to fulfill their destiny, to live more authentic and more joyful lives, and, by doing so, to gladden the heart of the God who made them.

It is clear that many of the distinctives of such a model — nontechnological farming, craftsman production, division of daily activities between labor and study — would require a drastically different attitude toward time than that which holds in our present society. Viewed from our perspective, deliberately "old fashioned" agricultural methods are time-consuming and "non-productive," craftsmanship is inefficient, and the hours of most people's days are too short to "waste" on reflection. Yet for Maurin and the Catholic Worker, time — like every other of God's creatures — is holy; but its holiness is lost when we fill it with a rush of activity, distract ourselves from its movement by numbing diversions, or treat it as simply one more thing to be bought and sold ("time is money" was a business slogan that particularly offended Maurin). In the inevitable slowing of the pace of life that would come in such a community as Maurin proposed, we would be brought back in touch with the sacredness of our labor, our study and our play; we would enter into a new relationship with time in which there could be found healing for spirit, mind and body alike. Paradise, while not fully regained, might at least be glimpsed in its remnant outline, visible beneath the redeemed patterns of everyday life.

Cultivation

A final and vital component of the sort of community Maurin envisioned is represented by the third of his alliterative triad of "cult, culture and *cultivation*." Maurin's village community would have a connection with the soil, with the natural cycles of the seasons, with planting, springing to life, harvesting, death and decay. We are, Maurin insisted, not fully human without a fruitful relationship with the earth, a relationship that reflects the ontological truth expressed through the Genesis myth of God's placing Adam and Eve in a garden with the mandate to till and tend it.

While Maurin unapologetically drew this principle from the specifics his own peasant background, he was adamant that the call to an agriculturally-based life was a fundamental issue of human nature in general. Not every person might be primarily a farmer, but — in a distributist commune on the land — every person would in some way play a significant part in the holy process by which we plant seed in the earth; nurture, cultivate and water the plant; harvest its fruit; grind and bake grain for bread; crush and ferment fruit for wine; consume and share food with each other to nourish life; and then defecate back into the earth to enrich it for the next round of planting.

This grounding in the natural cycle of life is important for several reasons. It teaches us a proper humility regarding our place in creation: We may be "a little lower than the angels," but our bodies will eventually feed the earth as well. It guards us from a false dualism that would divorce spirit from matter, limiting God's activity to the former and attributing evil to the body and the material world. It keeps us in touch with the glory to be found in the messy, sticky, dirty, organic natural things which God made and pronounced good. And since farming, perhaps more than any other human endeavor, requires the cooperation of forces outside our control, it constantly reminds us of our ultimate dependence upon God.

In today's urbanized service and information society, when Western governments are busy encouraging industrial development in those remaining areas of the world where its ascendancy is incomplete, such a call to a rural agricultural life may seem quaint, romantic, even faintly ridiculous. But, it might well be asked, where has the alternative brought us?

Not long into the Industrial Revolution, the monstrous and dehumanizing character of the emerging modern city became a theme for poets, novelists and social critics. In his lament entitled "London," radical visionary William Blake alluded to the squalor, ugliness, filth, economic exploitation, violence, sensual corruption and disease that plagued that city in the eighteenth century, and — despite the sometimes heroic efforts of nineteenth and early twentieth century urban reformers and the purported protections of the modern welfare state — not that much appears to have changed. In their Houses of Hospitality and soup kitchens, Catholic Workers today see first hand, in a way few of us do, the brutal reality of metropolitan life as it is experienced by those who through poverty, disability, age, addiction or simple bad luck end up slipping through the cracks and onto the streets and alleys of the blighted central cores of the contemporary city.

But even for the more fortunate, the Worker would insist, urban life by its very nature conflicts with what we were created to be: By its size, it defeats community; by paving over the earth, it cuts us off from our necessary tie to productive work with the soil; by its frantic pace and endless diversions, it distracts us from our calling to conscious, intentional living. By its tolerance of vice, it tempts us to devalue the moral significance of our own lives and the lives of others; by its anonymity, it isolates us. For Maurin, the answer was simple. Just as the Industrial Revolution, however pervasive its effects, was to be rejected, so too was the city, however enticing its attractions.

There are at least two ironies here. First, for most people who are aware of the Catholic Worker, its connection with the inner city — the soup kitchen, the bread line — is a fundamental element of its character. Probably few who admire the movement from afar realize that at the core of its message is a call for return to the land.

Second, and more poignantly, even before she moved into a rented room on New York's Lower East Side in 1916, an ardent young socialist not yet twenty years old, Dorothy Day loved the ethnic diversity, energy and stimulation of the city. It was in the cities, New York in particular, that the passionate young radicals with whom she identified, many of them the sons and daughters of poor immigrants, were embracing revolution and bohemian renunciation of stultifying bourgeois values. To the end of her life, Day remained a profoundly urban person. Nonetheless, she — and the Worker after her — accepted Maurin's insistence that the end product of his green revolution would be distributist village communes on the land and, in the hope and promise of that eventuality, the Worker has over the years embarked on a number of experiments in farming, out of which have come some of the movement's most humorous anecdotes — at least if humor is, as sometimes claimed, "disaster recollected in tranquillity."

Provisional Steps

As visionary as his ultimate view might be, Maurin had a practical appreciation of the fact that not many of us have the resources to immediately set up a distributist community in the country. *He* certainly did not, the unemployed homeless to whom he first began proclaiming his message in the early 1930s did not, and neither, at the time of their fateful meeting in the fall of 1932, did struggling free-lance journalist and single mother Dorothy Day. Such lack of means did not signify that one was powerless to respond to the call of the green revolution, however — not given the personalist summons to immediate action wherever one is and with whatever one has at hand.

Accordingly, Maurin proposed three provisional steps that would prepare the way for and provide the means to the revolution that was to come: "clarification of thought" (by means of "roundtable discussions"), Houses of Hospitality, and "agronomic universities."

He set out this three-point program for immediate action in one of his "Easy Essays," printed in *The Catholic Worker*'s June, 1933, issue:

> We need round-table discussions
> To keep trained minds from becoming academic.
> We need round-table discussions
> To keep untrained minds from being superficial.
>
> We need Houses of Hospitality
> To give to the rich the opportunity to serve the poor.
> We need Houses of Hospitality
> To bring social justice back to Catholic institutions.
>
> The unemployed need food.
> They can raise that
> In an agronomic university.
> The unemployed need to acquire skill.
> They can do that in an agronomic university.

In these deceptively simple words lies the framework for nearly everything the Worker has done and been in the now more than sixty years that have followed.

Clarification of Thought

Maurin agreed with Lenin that "before you can have revolution, you must have a theory of revolution." Before you can act on reality, you must know what reality is. Since, in Maurin's view, we are all to a greater or lesser extent victims of the inescapable distortions by which our debased society legitimizes itself, we are all therefore in need of a new clarity of vision and understanding, so that we might better recognize the failures and brokenness of things as they are and better perceive the possibilities to which we are called by creation and grace.

It was only through such clarification, Maurin insisted — only through a growing understanding of what makes up a truly human life, only through hearing the "good news to the poor" proclaimed in all its fullness — that one could be liberated from the complex of lies buttressing the status quo. What Maurin termed "clarification," others might label propaganda (and even some friends of the Worker did so), but it was to his mind an essential prerequisite of personalist action for change.

How was such clarification to be achieved? First and foremost, by talk, something of which Maurin was extremely — some said inordinately — fond. He even had his own theory as to the appropriate style of discourse to be used: Rather than conventional dialogue or the give and take of debate, he favored a method apparently drawn both from his own rhetorical impulses and the techniques of the soapbox, where he gained his first audience among the drifting unemployed and homeless of the Great Depression. Put simply, it was that each speaker would talk for as long as he or she wished, without interruption, comment or question, saying everything on his or her mind. During this oration, the other participants were not to be thinking about their questions, disagreements or counter-arguments; rather, they were to put their whole energies to as fully as possible receiving and comprehending the message being conveyed by the one who held the floor. When one person finished speaking, the next would be afforded similarly undivided attention, until all had said everything that was on their minds and all had, presumably, benefited from the wisdom and insight of the others. Even one-on-one, this methodology held true for Maurin, as a Wall Street stockbroker who admired him noted: "He doesn't talk *with* you, he talks *at* you — as though he were addressing a mass meeting." Out of such "roundtable discussion," Maurin maintained, clarification would ultimately emerge and bear fruit — not by domination, persuasion or authority, but by the resonating witness of the Spirit working upon the human heart touched by truth. Or, as he put it much less abstractly: "I will give you a piece of my mind and you will give me a piece of your mind and then we both will have more."

Initial Worker forays into publicly advertised roundtable discussions met with less than resounding success. In an announcement in the second issue of *The Catholic Worker* which was reprinted in a mimeographed broadside and distributed in Union Square, Maurin optimistically invited "everyone ... Communists, radicals, priests ... laity." When the appointed Sunday afternoon arrived, however, only fifteen or twenty chairs were filled in a hall with seating for one hundred and fifty. This was the tally according to most sources, at any rate; Arthur Sheehan, always one to put the best face on anything, claims in his biography of Maurin that there were forty in attendance. Whatever the numbers, the discussion was dominated by a speaker from the floor who insisted that the Roman Catholic Church was inextricably fettered to the dying capitalist order. At another roundtable, things were thrown off track by the vigorous protests of an Irish laborer who noted that the Workers must all be Reds because not once during the entire evening had anyone said a word about the Blessed Virgin Mary.

Perhaps not surprisingly, unstructured open forums where anyone could speak at length tended toward confusion and lack of focus. Moreover, Maurin himself proved something of a problem. While Day and others in the Worker loved and venerated him as a teacher and prophet, outsiders often found his lengthy dissertations incomprehensible and tedious, if not comic, especially as they were delivered in a heavy and, to many, not particularly pleasant French accent. (Maurin's first language had not been French, but the Auvergne *patois* of his native Languedoc and that dialect still colored his speech patterns.) Indeed, even Dorothy Day had to admit that "he spoke with an accent so thick it was hard to penetrate to the thought beneath."

As a result, in relatively short time, roundtable discussions were replaced with more structured lectures, often by leading Catholic and progressive thinkers of the day. The first of these was given by a Columbia professor whose topic was ambitious, to say the least — nothing less than "The History of Nationalism." Subsequent presentations covered subjects ranging from "The Race Problem," to Judaic mysticism, to Scholastic Philosophy, with instructors drawn from the faculties of all the major area universities. As a growing audience of Catholic Workers, their unemployed guests from the streets, clergy and earnest young Catholic students squeezed into the movement's East 15th Street tenement office week after week for this "workers' school," it must have seemed that at least one element of Maurin's vision was truly being realized:

> The scholars must tell the workers
> > what is wrong
> > with the things as they are.
> The scholars must tell the workers
> > how things would be,
> > if they were as they should be.
> The scholars must tell the workers
> > how a path can be made
> > from the things as they are
> > to the things as they should be.

In a nod to Maurin's roundtable method, however, it remained a venerable Worker tradition, that — even in these more formal contexts — time be given to allow participants opportunity to respond and comment from the floor, not just ask questions.

It is perhaps not surprising, given Dorothy Day's background as a writer and sometime editor for radical newspapers like *The New York Call* and *The Masses*, that journalism was to be the other primary vehicle for Worker clarification of thought. At a penny a copy (and more often than not given away), *The Catholic Worker* was the voice of the movement. While Maurin apparently initially expected it to contain nothing more than his "Easy Essays" (which he had previously distributed in laboriously hand-copied or mimeographed form), under Day's editorship the paper immediately became something much more sophisticated, applying Catholic Worker principles to a myriad of social concerns. When Worker houses began springing up around the country in the years following the New York community's founding in 1933, it was often assumed that some sort of paper, however modest, was a necessary ingredient of any genuine Catholic Worker effort.

Houses of Hospitality

From the time Dorothy Day first began feeding Peter Maurin and his homeless friends around her kitchen table, hospitality has been a particular emphasis of Worker life. In a recent issue of *The Mustard Seed*, the journal of the Toronto Catholic Worker, that community spoke of hospitality as the movement's special charism; Day herself entitled one of her books simply *House of Hospitality*; and it was such Houses of Hospitality that were the second of Maurin's provisional steps toward the fullness of the green revolution.

Like everything else at the Worker, moving from principle to practice regarding hospitality was a matter of "small beginnings and learning by doing." Maurin had been advocating Houses of Hospitality in the pages of *The Catholic Worker* for five months before an "official" House was opened. What occasioned it was simple (and typical of the Worker's *ad hoc* approach): An unemployed young woman read what Maurin had written, took him at his word, and appeared at the paper's offices in October of 1933 asking for shelter. Within a few hours a nearby apartment had been rented with room for ten women. A house for men soon followed. Later moves brought guests and community members together under various roofs in Greenwich Village, Chinatown and the Lower East Side.

Hospitality, as understood and practiced by the Worker, differs from even the best of conventional social service in that, in true personalist fashion, it draws the needy into the privacy of one's own family, home, and table, thereby breaking down the protective distancing provided by more traditional "arm's length" charity. In so doing, it grants the recipient individual attention and recognition of his or her unique, irreplaceable value and, at the same time, allows the giver a humanizing, intimate involvement with the poor, who — as the Gospel and Christian tradition teach — are in a special way Christ present among us.

For both giver and recipient, hospitality offers opportunity for a genuine experience of love, since true hospitality is not just a matter of meeting physical needs for food or shelter, but rather of striving to create the "I-thou" relationship between people. In a world in which a primary wound in many lives is the lack of any sense of personal significance, such intentionality of focus may be the greatest gift that can be given, especially to those whose brokenness, whatever its form, makes them particularly unappealing to our natural inclinations. The fact that such "I-thou" hospitality is a costly, pain-filled (as well as blessed) task is one to which ample witness is borne in the history of the Worker itself.

Yet, Maurin insisted, it is a task to which all Christians (not just Catholic Workers) are called. Indeed, Maurin often spoke of Worker Houses of Hospitality as a temporary measure, one which the movement should be striving through its witness to render obsolete. He looked to the day when every Catholic home would have a "Christ room" where hospitality would be offered and every Catholic parish would provide accommodation for those without shelter or means of self-support. Until such time, however, Worker hospitality would welcome the poor and broken as brothers and sisters with rights of family to a place at the table. Workers would express God's self-emptying love through service that was neither faceless (as it is in bureaucracy), condescending (as is too often the case in traditional charitable work) nor couched in judgment (as is typical in the evangelical Skid Row mission).

With his usual enthusiasm, Maurin urged that Houses of Hospitality offer even more than shelter, food and personalist love. In one of his more ambitious "Essays," he itemized some of the other things Catholic Worker Houses might be: vocational training schools (including training for the priesthood!); Catholic reading rooms; catechetical schools; centers for roundtable discussions. In short, they would be places where "Catholic thought is combined with Catholic Action." And, Maurin insisted:

> Thought and action
> must be combined.
> When thought
> is separated from action,
> it becomes academic.
> When thought
> is related to action
> it becomes dynamic.

While no attempt was made to put some of Maurin's more ecclesiastically oriented proposals into practice (no doubt in part due to discomfort with their overtones of proselytism), the diversity of Catholic Worker "action" in the early days is remarkable — libraries, discussion groups, literacy classes, craft demonstrations, "worker schools." In a particularly telling example of the young movement's earnest piety, a Los Angeles House in the mid-1930s sought to uplift its residents' souls with a screening — on a sheet after dinner — of Cecil B. DeMille's silent epic "King of Kings."

Most Worker communities today would no doubt recoil from the more overtly "Catholic" of Maurin's suggestions. Nevertheless, a fruitful principle remains: There is no single, determinative model for the Worker's practice of Catholic action. In true personalist fashion, the particular and immediate circumstances of a given time and place determine what a House should do and be. While hospitality (food and shelter) are primary, further possibilities for enfleshing self-emptying love are as various as human need. A Catholic Worker House near an isolated federal penitentiary has offered temporary housing to prisoners' families unable to afford local motels, along with free child care during visits. A Worker community in an inner city neighborhood with a sudden influx of undocumented families from Central America opened an at-cost food store. Other communities have set up free clinics, free legal centers, children's day programs, draft resistance centers, needle exchange programs. But in every Catholic Worker House of Hospitality, the first and primary "dynamic action" toward Peter Maurin's ultimate vision of egalitarian communal life is taken as the affluent and the poor are brought together under one roof in a community where they can learn from each other, love each other, and enflesh in their new-found connection the embracing breadth of the coming Reign of God.

Agronomic Universities

The "agronomic university" was Maurin's somewhat grandiose appellation for what was to be better known as the Catholic Worker farm, of which there have been several examples over the years. As the last of Maurin's three provisional steps, such farms would admittedly fall far short of the distributist rural commune to which his vision aspired, but they were a seminal form of that goal, as well as a necessary first step toward it.

These farms would provide a place where city youth, long cut off from the agricultural arts, could learn the ways of the earth and be trained in the skills of farming and husbandry (hence the title "university"). In the more healthful environment of the farm, the psychic wounds of the poor could be healed through exposure to fruitful labor, country quiet and the rhythms of the seasons. Those too old to work could rest in the shade and share their wisdom with the young. Children could grow up unthreatened by the dangers and destructive temptations of the urban environment.

To be sure, certain of Maurin's more fanciful proposals for such farms can challenge one's tolerance. He was, for instance, apparently serious when he once suggested that Skid Row alcoholics be married to area prostitutes and that these couples then be shipped off to the bracing simplicity of the Catholic Worker farm where they might build new and better lives for themselves. And Worker lore is rife with tales of the catastrophic results of putting idealistic youth and the wounded urban poor together on the land with limited resources and little preparation or training. Nevertheless, if one considers today's city — its homeless, its gang-terrorized children, its elderly locked in moldering rooms in fear of the violence of the streets — one may well find new reason to respect Maurin's apparently simplistic nostrum.

If, as Maurin and the Worker teach, our ultimate good is best served in a craft and agricultural community on the land, then even preliminary, halting steps toward that end are surely steps in the right direction. The sometimes humorous failures of Catholic Worker experiments in farming do not detract from the significance of what was attempted.

Neither do these disappointments disprove the wisdom of Maurin's conviction that just as we are, in the symbolic language of Genesis, made *from* the earth and just as we will return *to* it in death, so we are created for a life-giving relationship *with* the earth without which we cannot be whole. The centrality of this conviction to Worker thought assures that — no matter how grounded in gritty urban reality its present forms of service might be — the movement will always look to the land as an ultimate goal, not only for its own members but for the poor whose wretchedness particularly cries out for the healing to be found in fruitful labor with the soil.

Chapter Five

Nonviolence and Resistance

The final major element of the Worker vision not only came close to destroying the movement in the 1940s but also has arguably brought it more forcibly to public attention in the last three decades than any other. It is an absolute, unwavering commitment to nonviolence and — the reverse side of the coin, as it were — to acts of resistance to the war-making state and the military-industrial complex which profits by the state's wars and preparations for war.

Peter Maurin himself said relatively little about nonviolence (or, as it was more often termed during his lifetime, pacifism). Yet there can be no doubt that he was, in fact, a pacifist by conviction — though he "did not engage in discussions on the morality of modern war but left that for others," according to Sheehan. (On the other hand, Sheehan also notes that when challenged with the age old question of what he would do if threatened by an armed attacker, Maurin's response was: "I would tell him, 'Shoot me if you will, but I will not shoot you.'")

From information given Sheehan by one of Maurin's brothers, it would appear that this pacifism resulted from Maurin's personal experience as a military conscript in 1898-99. In fact, there is evidence that the primary motivation for his emigration from his native France to Canada was an objection to continuing service in the military reserve.

Yet, according to Dorothy Day, in the reminiscence mentioned earlier, "Peter did not want to be fragmented by being labeled pacifist or anarchist. First of all, we are Catholics." William Miller may have caught the spirit of Maurin's commitment to nonviolence best when he wrote: "Peace was so profoundly and integrally at the center of his vision that he did not have to particularize about it."

Indeed, nonviolence was central to Maurin's thought — an inescapable consequence of the spiritual significance his green revolution

gave to each human will and its decisions. Violence in any form subjects that will to coercion, thus blocking the possibility of authentic
moral choice. Genuine *metanoia* is unlikely at the business end of a
gun. In fact, the damage its violence would do to human moral freedom was one of Maurin's chief objections to the Marxist doctrine of
class warfare. Oppressive political structures might, at least in the
short term, be changed, but hearts would not, and without changed
hearts structural reform would not last. Even the most utopian social
organization would be destroyed from within if it were driven to defend itself from the ongoing subversion of those on whom it had been
imposed by force.

As for more conventional wars between nations, these in general
lack even the commendable *goals* of revolutionary conflict. Further-
more, any violence, offensive or defensive, brings objectification of
those we name "the enemy." Yet our enemies too, no matter how profound their evil in our eyes, are beloved children of God, made in the
divine image. They, too, are of inestimable value. Peter Maurin's vision encompassed all this, but his chosen emphasis lay elsewhere. As
a result, it was Dorothy Day, not Maurin, who gave consistent voice
in the Worker movement to an unconditional dedication to the principle and practice of nonviolence.

Day had been a pacifist before her conversion. With her fellow
turn-of-the-century radicals, she saw modern warfare as the slaughter
of workers for the profit of industrialists, international financiers and
munitions manufacturers. After she became a Christian, she changed
the basis but not the substance of her commitment to nonviolence.
Perhaps reacting somewhat defensively to fellow-Catholics who dismissed her pacifism as nothing more than a vestige of her former socialist convictions, Day wrote: "My absolute pacifism stems purely
from the gospel teaching."

As she would write extensively in the following years, Day saw
clearly that the message of Christ — once read without the interpre-
tative grid of the Church's later "just war" theory — was unambigu-
ous on the issue. Further, Christ's own example in giving up his life
on the cross evidences the fact that self-emptying love is to be expressed not through violence or the imposition of power, but rather
through redemptive self-sacrifice. The fact that the earliest Christians
had, for several centuries, been unanimous in their rejection of participation in war, along with the subsequent long history of alternative
witness within the Christian tradition, exemplified by the Anabaptists

and Quakers of the radical Reformation, supported Day's certainty that to follow Christ faithfully was to embrace the role of peacemaker which he had enjoined as "blessed."

It was theological folly, Day maintained, to insist that as individuals we are called by Christ to turn the other cheek when attacked, and then to argue that — once we are decked in the authority of the state — this obligation is somehow annulled. No nation, no political system, no power alliance is so important as to release us from our primary moral obligations to each other or justify our violating the sanctity of another human life. Perhaps her definitive word, the final basis of her unstinting commitment to nonviolence, is to be found in the simplicity of an undated note from one of her journals (the emphases are hers): "I do not believe people can fight with *love*, with *charity.*" Since Day knew, as St. John of the Cross had taught, that "love is the measure" by which all things are to be judged, that was for her enough to enjoin those who would follow Christ from participation in any form of violence.

Worker convictions regarding nonviolence were first put to test in the fire of passions roused in this country by the Spanish Civil War of the mid-1930s. Day's old friends on the left were united in their outrage when Nazi Germany and Mussolini's Italy aggressively intervened in support of Generalissimo Franco's insurgent fascists as they smashed a democratically elected and reforming republican government so as to maintain the power and privileges of the aristocracy, the military and a conservative Church. Many progressives joined battalions of the International Brigades and went to Spain to fight alongside the Republicans. On the other hand, most of the Worker's Catholic supporters (of whom there were many, both lay and clerical, in the first years of the movement) were just as committed to the cause of Franco. In their view the conflict was nothing less than an apocalyptic battle between atheistic, Bolshevik-inspired enemies of Christ's Church and modern-day knights of the cross fighting to defend her, an interpretation of the conflict heavily promoted by the American hierarchy and the Catholic press in this country through sensationalized reports of priests being shot, nuns violated and churches razed.

While Day's instinctive sympathies certainly lay with the Republicans (except for their anti-clericalism), she refused to support either the loyalist struggle against fascism or Franco's crusade for the old Catholic order, arguing instead in the pages of *The Catholic Worker* that both sides to the conflict were culpable. After prominent Catholic prelates in this country prayed publicly for Franco's success, she wrote that Catholic Workers were "not praying for victory for Franco. ... Nor are we praying for victory for the loyalists whose ... leaders are trying to destroy religion. We are praying for the Spanish people — all of them our brothers in Christ."

The result, not surprisingly, was that Day and the Worker were excoriated by both sides. The left saw the Worker's position as a jesuitical cover for clerical fascism and thus a betrayal of Republican martyrs to the cause of freedom. Many in the Church saw it as proof that the leopard indeed cannot change its spots and that Day and the Worker, despite their external trappings of Catholicism, were at heart one with the communists and other enemies of the Church that claimed its own martyrs in the struggle. With the left, Day lost much of whatever credibility she had maintained after her conversion; with Roman Catholics, she lost both moral standing and practical support. The number of subscriptions to *The Catholic Worker* declined significantly as many previous friends withdrew in painful disillusionment over what they saw as the movement's refusal to stand with the Church against the forces of anti-Christ.

If Dorothy Day's commitment to nonviolence in the context of the Spanish Civil war proved troublesome for supporters and critics alike outside the movement, her equally adamant pacifism in World War II rent the Worker within. It is probably difficult from the perspective of this more jaundiced, post-Vietnam age to adequately appreciate the overwhelming unanimity of national purpose that followed the "unprovoked" attack on Pearl Harbor and America's sudden entry into the conflict — or the effect of *The Catholic Worker*'s banner headline, just after the declaration of war, on American sensibilities in that very different time: "WE CONTINUE OUR CHRISTIAN PACIFIST STAND." For those on the left, one's duty was made clear by a fascist enemy and a newly forged alliance with the Soviet Union (still held by many to be the hope of the world, despite Stalin's depredations, which were generally unknown or discounted). Those on the right probably required no more than instinctive patriotism to support their government once it went to war, but the fact that the conflict had been instigated by expansionist conquest against non-belligerent sovereign states gave added moral credence to the righteousness of the national cause. The Catholic Church — long anxious to prove its "Americanism" in the face of chronic anti-Romanism and the immigrant taint which still attached to the Church in the popular mind — was quick to give its blessing to American involvement, despite the fact that the Holy Father had often spoken warmly of the fascists as the Church's best defense against the dangers posed by godless Communism.

Across the country, Worker communities were split between those who supported Dorothy Day's strict pacifism and those who felt this particular war was morally justifiable. Some stopped distributing *The Catholic Worker*. There were long hours of meeting and debate, with much pounding on tables. Financial support withered and many Houses were forced to close as the young Catholic Workers either left to join the armed forces (one writer estimates that fully eighty-percent of the movement's inductable men abandoned pacifism), perform noncombatant service, or enter conscientious objector camps or prison. Through it all, Dorothy Day held firm, even in the face of possibly justified charges of dictatorship and purging of dissidents after she sent a letter to all Worker houses stating that they must either distribute *The Catholic Worker* or disassociate themselves from the movement. By the end of the war, the Worker was only a shadow of its former self. In 1940 there had been more than thirty active communities; by January, 1945, only ten of these remained.

In the vicious anti-Communist fervor of the years that followed, the movement's identification with once admired but now damning leftist causes and principles further marginalized and isolated it, and when Peter Maurin died in 1949, an observer might have seemed justified in considering it only a matter of time until the Catholic Worker itself followed him into extinction. But the force of Maurin's vision and (in no small part) the holy intractability of Dorothy Day's will were not to be so easily quenched.

Mid-century, the movement was certainly smaller than it had been in the years of growth before the war — only eight communities were still in operation by 1950 — and far less "respectable." Dorothy Day and the Worker were frequently the target of condescending comment, if not outright hostility, from the Catholic press. After she appeared on the platform with known communists at a New York rally of the "communist-front" National Council of Arts, Sciences and Professions, Day was pilloried in a nationally syndicated column for diocesan newspapers as lacking common sense, committing a "monumental blunder," acting in a manner "silly beyond words," and limiting her "bleeding heart" to leftist stereotypes while betraying the victims of

Communist "blasphemies ... sacrileges ... [and] horrible lies." Following the Vatican excommunication of communists in the summer of 1949, the Worker was also at least indirectly rebuked from the pulpit of St. Patrick's Cathedral, when a homilist lashed out at the fellow-traveling, "duped ... so-called idealist Christian Left" in a sermon delivered in the presence of Cardinal Spellman and understood to carry his *imprimatur*. Despite all this and much more, however, it was in the politically stifling decade of the 1950s that the Worker forged the model of self-sacrificial resistance that was ultimately to be perhaps its most notable characteristic in the latter third of the century and a source of renewed growth for the movement with the rise of the "New Left" that coalesced around opposition to the Vietnam War in the 1960s.

While Maurin often spoke of the Worker call to be "announcers not denouncers," Dorothy Day had a good deal of the denouncer in her temperament and she was no stranger to civil disobedience or its consequence, incarceration. While still in her teens she had been arrested with demonstrating suffragists outside Woodrow Wilson's White House (even though she herself, as a philosophical anarchist, did not support the goals of the suffrage movement, as already noted, believing far more fundamental changes were required). A second period in jail a few years later was not the result of any act of public resistance — she was picked up in a sweep of an I.W.W. house where she'd gone to visit a troubled friend. Nonetheless, her experience of that imprisonment would later figure largely in her understanding of jail time as a contemporary method for practicing the traditional work of mercy of "visiting the prisoner."

Despite this history, however, until the early 1950s the Worker had focused its commitment to nonviolence on the written word and support of individual acts of conscience, as when a handful of members and friends of the movement were jailed as pacifists during the war years. What public action there was had generally been limited to picketing. It was the awesome, diabolic power unleashed at Hiroshima and Nagasaki, and the arms race that followed, which spurred Dorothy Day and the Worker to a new, more active form of witness for nonviolence in the following decade. That, and the arrival of Ammon Hennacy at the Worker.

Hennacy's chief contribution to the movement's more activist approach to nonviolence was his enthusiastic practice and promotion of civil disobedience as a tool of personalist revolution. Making something of a career of public fasting and symbolic action as tactics for confronting what Dorothy sometimes referred to as "Holy Mother State," Hennacy insisted that one must act — alone if necessary, even at the risk of appearing foolish or mad — but always *act* upon the truth. For Hennacy, there were no excuses for anything less than full-fledged, immediate engagement with the status quo in all its diabolical manifestations. As Dorothy Day wrote in 1956, "to Ammon, this whole lifetime is a time of crisis." It was at his suggestion that Dorothy Day and other Catholic Workers and supporters were arrested over several consecutive years in the mid-1950s for refusing to take cover during New York's annual city-wide civil defense drills, and Hennacy's continuing legacy can be perceived in thirty years of Worker symbolic witness against the bomb, Vietnam, abuse of migrant farm workers, American intervention in Central America and the nuclear arms race.

The other principal contributor to the Worker's developing understanding and practice of nonviolence during the middle years of the century could hardly have presented a greater contrast to Ammon Hennacy. As quiet and reflective as Hennacy was loud and brash, Robert Ludlow had been a conscientious objector during World War II and came to the New York House shortly after the war. In a number of thoughtful articles for *The Catholic Worker* during the late 1940s and early 1950s, Ludlow attempted to forge a more conceptually defensible foundation for Catholic Worker anarchism and pacifism. (In fact, the passionate near-poetry and dense intellectual rigor of some of his writing led Dorothy Day to admit to difficulties in following it).

As documented by Mel Piehl, it was Ludlow who first introduced into Worker discussion Gandhi's principles of passive resistance, according to which one opposes injustice and the violence of power by means of disciplined, nonviolent struggle most perfectly expressed through voluntarily accepted, transformative suffering. At the core of such action, Gandhi taught, is a passionate commitment to the sanctity of every life and a determination never to forget or disregard the essential humanity of one's opponent. Such a vision is clearly analogous to the example and teaching of Jesus and it found a ready response in the Worker movement, where it has formed the basis of a method of direct action and prophetic social witness which infuses the simple directives of gospel pacifism with the complementary principles of Gandhian nonviolence.

Catholic Worker resistance is grounded in its understanding of how the Christian is called to deal with evil. The self-emptying love to which each of us is summoned, the Worker insists, by its very nature excludes the possibility of doing violence, even when one is in the right (who, after all, was more "right" than Jesus?). Self-emptying love must, instead, overcome evil by taking that evil onto itself, suffering it, bearing its force to the utter extremity, so as to resurrect it to ultimately greater good, just as Jesus did.

Yet, the Worker affirms, such a Christ-like pattern is not passive or helpless in the face of evil. It is nonviolent, but it is *resistance* nonetheless, as Gandhi made clear. It is active, engaged. It avoids the tragic internal inconsistency of the world's attempts to defeat evil on its own terms and by its own means, however, attempts which inevitably end up perpetuating (even enlarging) the very evil against which one was fighting in the first place. Through nonviolent resistance, we soak evil up like a sponge, bearing its outrages, hoping always for the redemption of those who perpetrate it. Our goal is never just righting the wrong; we seek a change of heart in the wrongdoer as well, because he or she is also — at least potentially — our brother or sister in Christ, beloved by God.

Worker resistance at times has entailed Direct Action to stop the effect of evil. During the Vietnam war, for example, Catholic Worker "resistance centers" provided sanctuary and means of travel to Canada for "draft dodgers" and AWOL conscientious objectors. More often, however, given the enormity of the institutions and structures being addressed, such resistance has taken the form of symbolic actions that look to a more incremental movement toward the good.

When Catholic Workers keep vigil outside a nuclear test site, or accept arrest for climbing its fences, they are under no illusion that such actions will, in and of themselves, immediately defuse the weapons of mass destruction against which their witness is borne. Yet such resistance is more than empty theatrics — it is premised on the belief that conversion is possible, that the human heart can be moved by the grace of God to change, and that perhaps one of the most powerful inspirations for such change is an act of conscience, made on personal responsibility and at personal risk. Just as "the blood of martyrs" was once the "seed of the church," so these often less costly but no less real contemporary martyrdoms can be the seeds of reflection, new insight, transformation. And even if a "failure" in terms of putting an immediate end to the evils it confronts, such resistance is, for the

Catholic Worker, the inevitable and necessary consequence of choosing to live faithfully to the truth.

While a temptation to self-righteousness or the "martyr complex" always lurks in such a life of prophetic witness, at its best Catholic Worker resistance avoids easy rhetoric or the demonization of those it must oppose. When true to its vision, its sacrificial resistance is undertaken with that necessary humility which stems from recognition of one's own brokenness and sin. Embracing the counsel of Christ not only to love our enemies but also to pray and do good for them, Catholic Workers, as they resist the systemic evils of their generation, acknowledge that the "enemy" is passionately loved by God and a sacred bearer of God's image. Recognizing humankind's solidarity in grace as well as sin; they dare to believe that for the enemy, as for themselves, the promise of the triumphant Lord holds true and unchanging: "Behold, I am making all things new."

Chapter Six

"You Can't Repeal the Industrial Revolution"

John Cort, an early Catholic Worker stalwart who later left the movement and went on to found the Association of Catholic Trade Unionists, once said apropos the Worker vision which he could no longer share: "You can't repeal the Industrial Revolution." This is perhaps the most succinct expression of a view that prevails among many whose esteem for the Worker's sacrificial witness and life of service among the poor is mixed with a healthy dose of skepticism regarding the larger theoretical construct upon which that life is based.

For most of us, it is hard not to admire those who pour themselves out in intimate service to the very people we spend a good deal of effort keeping at the periphery of our lives and consciousness. (Worker legend recounts how one *grande dame* fan of Dorothy Day's swept into the New York house and — to Dorothy's deep chagrin — waxed effusive over Day's living "here, like this, among these *creatures!*") Even those who accused Catholic Workers of being communist dupes in the 1950s generally had to admit appreciation of their earnest embrace of the works of mercy. If one's politics are progressive, the movement's forthright stands against injustice and war will likewise earn respect. But to argue that the entire course of Western civilization for the last three hundred years has been a colossal blunder which must be rejected if we are to move toward spiritual and psychological wholeness may strike many as going too far.

It is certainly true that Maurin's admiration for pre-industrial peasant culture tended toward idealizing oversimplification (although he was hardly alone in this — it was a conceptual flaw shared by many in distributist and arts and crafts circles). He was, as well, clearly mistaken in his belief that workers and the poor would be quick to respond to the personalist message. A few did, but most "converts" to the Worker vision — once the Great Depression was over — were university educated young people from middle-class backgrounds. Further, it cannot be denied that, as a friend of the Worker once observed, "Peter Maurin went looking for a model of the ideal man and found himself — the peasant scholar."

Perhaps more to the point, Maurin's hope of a green revolution "growing up in the shell of the old" has not been realized in sixty years and would appear to have precious little likelihood of taking place at any point in the foreseeable future, as the "shell of the old" constantly finds new and more pernicious ways to reinvent itself. If it *can't* happen, one might argue, is there is any real point in arguing it *should* happen? Would we not be better off devising a program of moderate reform that takes into account and accommodates (even builds upon what is good in) the reality of the post-industrial age?

Of course, seen from the perspective and based upon the values of our world, such an argument makes eminently good sense. But, the Worker would respond, surely it is that very perspective and those very values that are part of the problem. The fact that humankind has corrupted itself beyond apparent power of remedy in no way invalidates God's original purposes in our creation. Jesus refused to accommodate the purported "realities" of life in the absolutism of his teaching ("... if your eye offends you, pluck it out"). He looked toward and called us to what is ultimately real, and in the same way the Worker dares to believe that one not only can but *must* strive to determine what is true and then live by it to the best of one's ability no matter what the consequences. Which brings us back to "holy failure" and a willingness to look beyond the limits of time for the ground of our action and our hope.

But for those who still cannot be convinced of the value of giving one's life to a program that, at least in immediate terms, "can't work," Maurin had an answer. To a newspaper editor who insisted that, rather than going back to the land, what one should be doing is working toward reforming industrial society so as to make it more Christian, Maurin replied with customary humility: "If you believe that can be done, then that is your task." Peter Maurin, however, and the Worker after him, do not believe it can be done, at least to any extent sufficient to heal the grievous wounds industrialism inflicts on the soul. Therefore, the Worker movement has opted for the seemingly far more ambitious, and yet in fact much simpler, approach of abandoning the failed industrial (or, now, post-industrial) model for one that better reflects the needs of the human spirit. If we are to pursue folly, they seem to say, it may as well be the folly of hard truth. Yet even "liberal" efforts toward partial amelioration are better than placid acceptance of, and benefit from, the status quo. What is absolutely unacceptable is to do nothing. As Maurin put it: "things are not good enough to be left alone."

The difficulty, even the seeming impossibility, of the green revolution ever achieving widespread realization does not — at least from a Christian perspective — necessarily invalidate that revolution's claims. Similarly, the repeated instances in which the Worker movement or its members could not or did not live up to the exacting standards of personalist action do not prove that Maurin's vision was erroneous.

There have been many such instances, to be sure. In the early years, even some of Day's most faithful supporters felt she too easily lapsed into the objectifying rhetoric of class warfare in the pages of *The Catholic Worker*. Some cringed when she wrote of the international financier Morgans gleefully contemplating the blood money they could make on preparations for war in Europe. Others were uncomfortable with a published censure of "Andy Mellon fight[ing] to hang onto [a] few million dollars of his $181,000,000 fortune" while striking employees of his National Biscuit Company were paid 22½¢ an hour — a rather mild rebuke, actually, compared to the invective that has appeared from time to time in the pages of other Worker communities' papers in subsequent decades.

Later, in her period of deep involvement with the Jansenist-tinged "Basic Retreat" during World War II, Day briefly abandoned her commitment to Maurin's decentralist rural commune, proposing that the Worker farm be turned into a retreat center. When confronted with this defection from the ultimate goal of the green revolution, she boldly proclaimed in the pages of *The Catholic Worker*, "We have failed," and went right on with her plans (which in the end were never fully realized).

In 1959, when Castro's rebels rose up in Cuba, Day and other writers for the paper were enthusiastic about the overthrow of Batista's notoriously corrupt regime. This enthusiasm led Day to perhaps her most conspicuous stumble, when, in attempting to explain her support of Castro's revolution despite its violence and increasing repression, she wrote that since Castro fought on behalf of the poor, if the Worker had to chose between the violence done to those poor by oligarchy and capitalist greed or Castro's violence aimed at liberating the poor, the Worker would choose the latter: "We do believe that it is better to revolt, to fight, as Castro did with his handful of men ... than do nothing." Former *Catholic Worker* contributor (and editor) Robert Ludlow was only one of many who wrote to the paper questioning why — after maintaining throughout World War II that force against the Nazis could not be morally justified — Dorothy Day now appeared ready to abandon her absolute commitment to pacifism.

Despite these and countless other, less public, failures to live up to its message, the Worker has pressed on, always imperfectly, but continuing to allow the claims of Maurin's magnificent vision to direct, challenge, rebuke and console it. Admirers, including some who write about the movement, often seem anxious to cast it in the role of a holy remnant, the radically faithful soul of a carnal, compromising Church. Another venerable Worker story recounts a pious lady asking Dorothy Day if, as is presumably customary with the uniquely holy, she had "visions" — to which Day replied "Hell, yes. Visions of unpaid bills." Stanley Vishnewski, longtime participant in the New York Worker, perhaps said it best: "They came expecting saints; they found human beings. And it was a great pity that none of us could measure up to their ... dreams of us."

In this regard, it should be remembered that Jesus called his followers to enact absolute self-emptying love in the daily choices of their lives, insisting that, by such love, "all will know you are my disciples." Yet even a superficial perusal of nearly two millennia of Christian history confronts us with the disheartening reality of how rarely such love has been the norm among those calling themselves Christians. Does that mean Jesus was mistaken? That his call was inadequate to the practical demands and constraints of the "real world?"

For any Christian, given the sorry "success rate" for the good news proclaimed by Jesus, determinations as to what is real, what is worth giving one's life to, cannot be based on calculations of potential or actual achievement. The victories of grace are small and often go unnoticed, matters more of slow process than spectacular result. What is important in them is as much the attempt as the thing accomplished. To argue that Maurin's vision must be faulty because it seems impossible to fulfill is to misunderstand a fundamental Christian mystery — that God works perfection through our brokenness, holiness through our sin, and the victories of eternity through our temporal fumblings and defeats.

"The problem with Peter's message," Dorothy Day once said, "Is that it is too simple." One can't help suspecting that it was not the message that was simple so much as the aphoristic, homely form in which Maurin chose to communicate it, but if Peter Maurin's message is "too simple," the gospel is too simple as well. That does not mean either is untrue.

Like Jesus, Maurin held up what we may too easily dismiss as an "ideal": nothing less finally than the Eternal Reign of God itself, the city in which there is no night, the high hill to which all nations come, breaking their swords into plowshares, the new heaven and earth. Even if such a model is no more than a beacon toward which we spend a lifetime striving, at least it assures, by its truth, that we are reaching in the right direction.

The Conflicting Values of Freedom and Unity

Another and perhaps more challenging critique of Maurin's vision would address not the difficulty of its achievement but the problems that would arise if it were somehow realized, even on a small scale. Clearly, the end of the green revolution — a self-contained rural community built upon common cult, culture and cultivation — is a profoundly conservative, homogeneous and, to some extent, *restrictive* construct for the social order. It is one in which any significant dissent from the corporate vision (which Maurin saw as being essentially theological — a "common cult") becomes intolerable.

No matter how sincere the attempt at mutual toleration and attentiveness to the voice of the Spirit in minority opinion, there can be little spiritually grounded accord in a community in which there exists significant divergence of conviction as to what spiritual reality *is*, or how it is to be faithfully applied (witness Dorothy Day's "dogmatism" regarding Worker pacifism in World War II). Maurin's ideal would seem to require — once a certain degree of fundamental disagreement has been reached, once the tensions of opposing beliefs and their practical application have been stretched to the breaking point — the expulsion of the dissenter; or, alternatively, an unthinkable, radical recreation of the core values and religious understandings of the community.

In a real sense, Maurin's model exemplifies a fundamental tension or paradox in the Christian understanding of life in this world. On the one hand, the Christian faith, by its premises, sees as the highest good a society reflecting what might be termed a theocentric unity, a society in which, in all its interrelationships, God's intent for justice, dignity, piety and righteousness are affirmed, practiced and enjoyed. When the Hebrew Scriptures speak of righteousness "exalting" a nation, they are not just saying that righteousness will give a nation a good reputation, but rather that the fullest chance for human joy and satisfaction will be found in a society grounded in a common appreciation for and practice of love, justice, mercy, nobility and truth. In such a society, common values would have their root in a common spiritual vision, and from the practical implementation of these values would flow continuity and order. In such a society, political and cultural issues would be in the most profound sense religious, since the very fabric of common life would be shot through with a unified theological understanding of the meaning, purpose and intended structure of that life. And this, of course, is exactly the sort of society toward which Maurin's green revolution looks.

In tension with this vision, however, is the fact that Christianity also affirms the absolute moral imperative of human freedom — intellectual, spiritual, and practical — not just because we *like* freedom, or at least the illusion of it (in fact, many times we do not, since freedom, by its nature, requires taking genuine responsibility for our lives — hence the eternal appeal of fascism), but because we are only fully human, fully what God intends us to be, when we act freely, without coercion.

The fundamental importance of our freedom is made clear in the most basic issue of human existence, our relationship with God. For a Christian, there is nothing more significant in any human life than the response to divine love, the love that is our source and purpose and only hope for true joy. Yet, God does not force that response, does not impose that love, because the only way it can be received and be true to itself is through its mirror, our free, grateful love in return.

If the single most important thing in our lives can only be had in the exercise of freedom, so with every other value: It is good that we should seek to know truth, but my truth imposed upon you defeats the moral and spiritual purpose of truth — the free, joyous assent of the will. It is good that we should live righteously, which is to say, live the truth, but your idea of righteousness enforced — with however good an intention — on my pilgrimage destroys any possibility of true righteousness in me, because even the most righteous act, if compelled against the will, is not righteousness at all, but hypocrisy.

For better or worse, it is this commitment to the inviolability of human freedom (within the bounds of respect for the rights and freedom of others) that is the ground of the pluralism of post-enlightenment democracies. And that pluralism is unmistakably the very secularization against which Maurin argued. It is the diametric opposite of theocentric unity.

In truth, both freedom and unity have their value. Each also has its pitfalls. The vision of theocentric unity offers precisely what our current culture so desperately lacks: a core of meaning and cohesion from which to act in harmony for each other's good, a source of common identity that can serve as a kind of psychic glue to hold us together and provide what is finally the only medium through which we can communicate intelligibly. Yet history shows the hideous dangers of the social organism built on a conviction of divine *imprimatur* — totalitarianism, writ large or small, seems the inevitable result.

Against that danger stands the ideal of freedom, the absolute right of responsible moral, spiritual and political choice which allows each person opportunity to determine what is of value, what is most fully human, what is to be sought and embraced. The fact is, of course, that freedom such as this is a rarity in even the ostensibly "free" democracies — it is denied to great numbers of their own citizens through economic and educational disenfranchisement, and in the Third World the greater powers pursue policies which expunge any hope of genuine freedom for millions.

And even at its best, the model of secular pluralism is not without its costs. Because we have grown up in a society that puts great rhetorical stock in freedom, we are sometimes less able to see the deleterious consequences of our pluralism than we are of culturally imposed conformity, but consequences there are: a lack of common values from which to seriously address any significant problem, a drift ever further and further apart into our special interest groups and subcultures (what sociologists have taken to calling the "tribalization" of the post-modern age), a continual erosion of any sense of personal identity with our culture or our past. And there is a particularly pernicious price exacted from the poor and the weak of our society: as whatever fragile thread there might be of connectedness with each other is snapped, they — the helpless and the broken — cease to have any claim on us. They are not *ours*, there is no authoritative, acknowledged voice to call us to responsibility for their needs.

Recognizing all these tragic tendencies, at least in seminal form, sixty years ago, Peter Maurin understandably emphasized the importance of restoring solidarity to society through commitment to the common good. But by incorporating into his vision for the ideal society both the value of freedom (through practical anarchism, whether or not he was willing to adopt the label "anarchist") and the value of theocentric unity (through common cult and culture), Maurin sought to bring these conflicting goods into balance. Whether he was entirely successful in that attempt is subject to debate. And if the tensions produced by embracing such paradox were not strain enough, there is, of course, the added reality that, even in a self-described anarchist community, freedom does not function within a psychological vacuum. In those Worker communities retaining the earlier model of spontaneously rising, self-validating leadership, there is the perpetual risk of direction by fiat or an "inner circle" of determinative authority that would seem decidedly at odds with the anarchist claims of the movement. On the other hand, more than one participant in Catholic Worker consensus has conceded that the process is subject to all the usual dynamics of peer pressure, manipulation, need for approval, and "group think."

Maurin appeared to believe that if men and women would draw together in the proper spirit of mutual submission, determined to enflesh self-emptying love in their dealings with each other, they could — on fundamentals at least — be of like mind. Out of such love and commonality of perspective would then come the means to resolve other, less critical matters. Short of the brief halcyon days of the earliest Jerusalem church (at least as that community is presented in St. Luke's idealized depiction in the Acts of the Apostles), such accord has been exceedingly rare in the Body of Christ. It has proved equally elusive for Catholic Worker communities. More often than not, the stronger personalities remain (Dorothy Day being the preeminent example), those opposing them leave — sometimes in anger or disillusionment, sometimes to found their own communities, sometimes as friends who take much from the Worker with them as they follow their own distinctive paths.

All the Way to Heaven

For those drawn by Maurin's eloquent vision of an existence more in harmony with creation's intent and responsive to the personalist call, the "harsh and dreadful" reality of daily practice in a Worker house can occasion a rude awakening. It is not just a matter of community being by its nature difficult and contrary to our natural selfishness, or of time and effort being required to wean oneself from the accustomed comforts and distractions of bourgeois life. It is not only that jail is tedious after the adrenaline rush of arrest. The true cost of faithfulness lies in the fact that the poor rarely resemble our pious fantasies of what they should be.

The actual poor exhaust us, exasperate us, disappoint and threaten us. They sometimes steal from us. They often bring pain and hopelessness and ugliness dead center into our lives. Once, when confronted yet again with the sometimes squalid chaos that life in a Worker house could become, Dorothy Day asked Peter Maurin plaintively if this were really what he'd envisioned the personalist revolution would be like. His only response: "At least it rouses the conscience."

And even when the poor do not disappoint us, even when the image of God in them bursts through with unmistakable clarity, to truly open ourselves to their suffering and sometime confusion and self-destructive compulsions is to be confronted inescapably with the bald fact of how very little control we truly have in this world. It is to come face to face with our smallness, our fragility. The poor strip away all our self-protective comfort (even the false comfort of piety); they frighten us, they frustrate us, they tear at our hearts.

The poor, more often than not, raise significant questions about even the legitimate hope we hold of Christ's redeeming presence in the world. In the midst of so much pain, for how long can it be enough to say that even the smallest personalist act of caring or compassion (a cup of water, a loving touch) has eternal cosmic meaning? How long before that truth sinks into mere wishful thinking, or the ersatz positive thinking of a commercial greeting card?

The answer, the Worker would respond, lies not so much in the occasional, though very real, triumph of grace (a healed body or mind, a "step up" out of the cycle of poverty) as it does in the very fact of participation in the lives of the poor. If, as Christians, our goal is to know and become more like the God we worship, then surely we are never so close to knowing the heart of God, never so close to reflecting the divine life, as we are when we sit helplessly in the midst of anguish and carry it, take it into ourselves, let our hearts be broken on the rack of human pain. For that is the mystery of deity that we proclaim in our Creed: that the Almighty by free choice abandons might and power and suffers with and in and through the creatures the divine heart loves more passionately than we can ever hope to love for all our commitment or caring.

In opening ourselves to the poor, the Worker affirms, we open ourselves as well to the terrifying mystery of our own mortality and to the self-imposed weakness of the God who made us. We open ourselves to the cross. We see control and power and positive thinking and optimism and the comforts of a false gospel slip through our fingers until we are finally left with only one thing: the raw fact that we are not alone in our terror and pain, our God is here with us, here perhaps as nowhere else. As the poor allow us to begin to touch this fundamental reality, we are paradoxically of all people most blessed, for it is only then that we begin to grasp and experience the remainder of the story: the Helpless One, nailed up and abandoned, sharing our despair ("My God, my God, why have you forsaken me?") is also the Exalted One whose victory begins not with resurrection three days later, but now, here, spiked up on wood, covered with blood and flies and spittle, naked in the blistering noonday sun. This moment of agony, spread out and woven into the whole course of human history is — as impossible as it may seem — the beginning of that new Eternal Reign of God where love is revealed for what it always has been, the life-pulse of the universe.

Inasmuch as we open ourselves to the poor (not only the poor in material things, but all the other poor who make up the "least" of Christ's promise), we begin not only to serve Christ, but to *know* Christ. Inasmuch as we allow their pain to get inside us, we begin to break open our safe hearts so the seed of true gospel hope might be planted. There are no shortcuts, no easier ways. As one young Catholic Worker used to quote the old evangelical saw of his childhood: "If you don't bear the cross, then you can't wear the crown." Not because one is given in payment for the other, but because the cross, being the ensign of the Lord, is the only crown worth wearing, in fact, the only real crown there is. Inasmuch as we allow ourselves to embrace and embody the helplessness of the poor as our own, the

Worker proclaims, we share the gift of that cross and — in the trust we call faith — the crown it is and will become forever.

It is in light of this truth that we can perhaps begin to fathom Dorothy Day's at first glance inexplicable fondness for St. Catherine of Siena's affirmation that "all the way to heaven is heaven." Day's journals make inescapably clear just how painful her struggle for faithfulness could be. As she contends with the woundedness of the poor, the occasional madness and violence of those she brings into the intimacy of her own home, the failures of community members to live up to the personalist vision, the attacks of disillusioned former Workers, the untimely deaths of those to whom she gave her great heart, the unreasonable demands of supporters, the opposition of critics, the seemingly incorrigible evils of the "filthy, rotten system" and — not least — the enduring cross of her own strong will, Day's life can often sound more like hell than heaven. Similar stories could no doubt be told by nearly every person who has embraced a Worker life over the past sixty years. And yet she often repeated St. Catherine's confession: "... *all* the way ..."

To understand how this could represent anything more than pious fancy, one must no doubt take into account Day's remarkable capacity for finding and rejoicing in beauty even in the midst of confusion and pain. Her columns for *The Catholic Worker* again and again reflect her delight in small things — a flowering tree, the smell of tomatoes as they grow, the daily rhythm of prayer and service. While she more than once quoted Ruskin on the *"duty* of delight," Day seems to have been blessed with a congenital ability to draw happiness from the simple gifts of life. And, of course, Maurin's vision, however incomplete the Worker's realization of it might be at any point in time, is itself a daring attempt to live out as much of heaven's reality as is possible *now*, in the conditions of this broken world. In a distributist commune on the land, Maurin taught, daily life would allow a foretaste of the joy that was always intended and is to be.

Yet these things alone hardly seem enough to warrant a claim that Dorothy Day's pilgrimage, or the journeys of so many others in the Worker movement, were themselves a part of the very fabric of the heaven that is to come. Rather, the truth of that astounding assertion surely lies in something deeper, lies in the fact that Dorothy Day, Peter Maurin and the Catholic Worker movement they created understand that, in accepting personalist responsibility to imbue their world with self-emptying love, in taking on the hard work of building true community, in making prophetic witness against the distortions and false gods of the culture, and — most importantly — in opening their lives to real friendship with the poor, they are placing themselves in the sacred place of encounter with the Holy One who was, who is and who always will be the reality of heaven. By seeking and serving Christ in his poor, by following Christ in small daily ways to his cross, the Catholic Worker affirms that it discovers not only an authentically human way of living but the One who is the source and end of such life as well. In that discovery — whatever its cost, even if apprehended more in stubborn faith than present experience — lies all the glory of heaven spread out like a banquet, inviting us, as the Psalmist chanted, to "taste and see how good the Lord is."

In such a life, received joyfully as a gift of love, all the way to heaven is heaven indeed.

Afterword

If, as I note in an earlier chapter, it is a dangerous thing to speak for the Catholic Worker dead, it is also surely a perilous undertaking to attempt articulation of the vision of a movement which has, over the years, so determinedly refused to be tied down to any binding, definitive statement of its tenets. One does well to remember what Peter Maurin always insisted: "... there is no party line at the Catholic Worker."

While I have attempted to deal honestly with the sources, in particular the written witness of Peter Maurin and Dorothy Day, some in the Worker may find themselves in disagreement with the emphasis I give (or fail to give) to particular aspects of the "Worker idea." Despite aspirations to objectivity, it is obvious that my personal sense of the Catholic Worker must color the perspective from which I view and interpret the principles and meaning of the movement. That sense is the result not only of my experience in the Los Angeles community, but also of the unique issues and preoccupations of my own history, both before and after my years as a "practicing" Catholic Worker. When Dorothy Day was criticized for residual class war attitudes, she often quoted St. Augustine: "[T]he bottle always smells of the liquor it once held." This holds true, surely, for each of us and — for myself — there is no language, no paradigm, other than that of theology through which the profound spiritual meaning of the movement can be understood.

Nonetheless, I must admit — with a certain chagrin — that the very attempt to write "theological reflections on the Catholic Worker" runs decidedly contrary to the fact that, as Arthur Sheehan notes in his biography, Peter Maurin "always shied away from theological terminology, for he knew very well what unattractive, pietistic connotations it had for many people." Despite Maurin's perhaps legitimate hesitations about over-spiritualizing his message, however, the fact remains that the goal of the movement — as often stated in *The*

Catholic Worker — is "to realize in the individual and society the expressed and implied teachings of Christ."

Yet it is also true that many who have been part of the Worker over the years have not considered themselves Catholic, or Christian, or even "religious" at all, at least in any conventional sense. As Dorothy Day once told Robert Coles in an interview: "... we are not asking people to fill out membership cards here, and we're not interested in declarations of religious affiliation." By defining the movement's significance as essentially theological, I in no way mean to diminish or ignore the participation and contribution of many who have served with the Worker — longer and no doubt far better than I — out of convictions different than my own.

The Christian, of course, may well affirm that, despite disavowals of religious motive, such committed men and women are responding to the Spirit of God. Dorothy Day certainly believed this to be the case, not only with "non-believing" Catholic Workers but also with many of her longtime friends on the left. As she told Coles:

> The longer I live, the more I see God at work in people who don't have the slightest interest in religion and never read the Bible and wouldn't know what to do if they were persuaded to go inside a church. I always knew how much I admired certain men and women (my "radical friends") who were giving their lives to help others get a better break; but now I realize how spiritual some of them were, and I'm ashamed of myself for not realizing that long ago. ...

Nevertheless, Day also recognized that speaking in such terms can run the risk of sounding smug to those who do not share one's faith — as if the underlying attitude were something along the lines of "even without knowing it, you are with us, which proves that we have been right all along." But this, of course, is not what she was saying. Such triumphalism was foreign to her nature. Rather, just as she saw the face of Christ in the faces of his poor, so she saw the self-emptying love of God at work in any selfless human action of compassion or caring, any human striving for justice or a better world. And seeing it, she could only rejoice.

All the same, she was straightforward in her insistence that the Catholic Worker was an unapologetically Christian enterprise. "We are here to bear witness to our Lord," Coles records her as saying. "We are here to follow His lead. We are here to celebrate Him through these works of mercy." And also:

> There is no point in trying to make us into something we are not. ... We feed the hungry, yes; we try to shelter the homeless and give them clothes, if we have some, but there is a strong faith at work; we pray. If an outsider who comes to visit doesn't pay attention to our praying and what that means, then he'll miss the whole point of things.

If such a statement hints of sectarian narrowness to some, it should be noted that Day chose "All is Grace" as the title for a book which she began but never finished on the spirituality of the Worker movement. For her, all that is good and beautiful and true was a gift of grace, whether it came through the community of faith or from outside it. God, she knew, is larger than our categories. God's love is without boundary. God's wisdom knows the human heart better than we can ever know even ourselves, much less one another. For Dorothy Day, affirming the work of the Spirit in the communist, the atheist or the searching young Catholic Worker in no way disparaged the intellectual integrity of those who could not share her beliefs. It merely expressed in yet another way her profound awareness of that intimate, imminent, on-rushing Love that — as she knew by both faith and experience — pulses within every atom of the universe, seeking always to heal, renew and make whole.

To come back once again to the fact of that Love — the foundational assumption of the Worker vision on which all else builds — brings me to the first of two additional matters which, in the course of the writing, have seemed again and again to fall outside the natural boundaries of the main chapters yet nevertheless to deserve comment. While they may prove to hold more particular interest to those close to the movement, they are relevant to any theological inquiry into the Worker and its meaning.

The Basic Retreat

Some who have followed the Catholic Worker over the years may wonder how I could write so much about its theology and say so little about the "Basic Retreat" that played such an important role in the spiritual development of Dorothy Day and others in the Catholic Worker during the grim years of World War II. After all, Day herself wrote that it was only through these retreats — led first by Josephite Father Pacifique Roy and later by Father John Hugo — that she discovered the delight and joy in her faith which she had expected, but not initially found, when she became a Catholic.

Day often wrote that "the only solution is love," and it was certainly through the retreats that she became convinced to her depths that the continuing incarnation of self-emptying love lies at the heart of the Christian's (and therefore the Catholic Worker's) calling. As Jim Forest notes in his biography of Day, central to the Basic Retreat teaching was the insistence that "every word, every thought, every action should be infused with God's love." Dorothy herself wrote, in a recollection of Fr. Roy after his death, "He convinced us that God loved us. ... He made us know what love meant, and what the inevitable suffering of love meant. ... He made us feel the power of love, he made us keep our faith in the power of love."

Despite this moving tribute, and the witness of a number of observers to the profound change in Dorothy's spirit as a result of the retreats ("she became holy," one is quoted as saying), I suspect that a tendency in the Retreat toward overemphasizing the "inevitable suffering of love" is what lay behind such troubling things as Dorothy's conviction that the best way to determine God's will in a particular situation is to look for that option which least appeals to oneself. Even she admitted that Fr. Roy could be "severe," and the retreats appear to have reflected, at least to some extent, a Jansenist repudiation of all natural good as an impediment to our calling to the higher, spiritual gifts of God. There was also some legalistic fussing over things like radios, lipstick and cigarettes. (Having said all that, we must admit that self-denial, self-discipline and an embrace of suffering for a higher good are concepts that war with the indulgent zeitgeist of our time and culture — which means they may very well be the very concepts we most need to hear forcibly proclaimed.)

Some in the movement who eagerly participated in the Retreat were apparently psychologically and spiritually wounded after the initial "rush" of the experience wore off in the dailiness of life among the poor. Gnostic divisions arose between those who had made the Retreat and those who had not. Most significantly, Catholic Worker artist Ade Bethune and others protested at the time that — in Fr. Hugo's teaching that "the best thing to do with the best things is give them up," for example — the Basic Retreat represented a deviation from Maurin's message, which celebrated the good gifts of the natural creation and our intended place in it. Even Day admitted in *The Long Loneliness* that, while "Peter always dealt with the things of this world ... Father Roy always dealt with the things of the next;" though she was quick to add: "The two were interwoven; time and eternity were one."

This turning away from the distinctiveness of Maurin's message is perhaps at the root of my disinclination to grant to the Retreat any lasting place in the ongoing development of the "Worker idea." Maurin was not a leading figure in the retreat movement within the Worker. This was surely due in great part to the fact that the Basic Retreat's emphasis on the exclusionary primacy of the spiritual over the material conflicted with his own understanding of the spiritual *redeeming* the material, of the material becoming the path to the spiritual through the restored social order of his personalist revolution. (There was also, of course, the problem of the Retreat being silent!)

The Role of Peter Maurin

Maurin's lack of involvement in the retreats raises yet another significant issue. Throughout the previous chapters I have attributed the substance of the Catholic Worker vision and way of life to him. That this could be a debateable point might seem surprising in light of Dorothy Day's perhaps overly self-effacing assertion, in a letter to an inquiring student, that "Peter Maurin is most truly the founder of The Catholic Worker Movement. I would never have had any idea in my head about such work if it had not been for him." Nevertheless, the precise nature of Maurin's contribution to the Worker idea has from time to time been disputed.

Many early Catholic Workers, supporting Day's view, perceived Maurin to be the dominant force in the movement. Julia Porcelli is quoted as describing him as a "voice of truth, of the Holy Spirit."

Arthur Sheehan — whose testimony Mel Piehl tends to discount in *Breaking Bread* on the ground that Sheehan "idolized" Maurin — wrote that "Peter was always a teacher ... dedicated, remarkable, of extraordinary scholarship. Yet all his learning and wisdom were seen through a peasant's eyes." A minority, however, shared the opinion of John Cogley, who insisted that Maurin's "intellectual genius was clearly exaggerated" and that he was "obviously uncomfortable" in the "feigned role of leadership," having nothing to contribute to a discussion unless the question at issue was "abstractly philosophical or sweepingly historical."

Piehl, perhaps to some extent reflecting the spirit of his times, tends toward the more skeptical, revisionist view. He refers to Day's building the "fiction" that the Catholic Worker was an attempt to realize Maurin's vision and suggests that Maurin's real significance was primarily symbolic. Peter, he argues, gave Day and the movement a connection to European Catholic intellectual culture, a male figurehead to satisfy the sexism of the Church, and a recognizable, living icon of traditional Catholic piety through his humble appearance and the purity of his single-mindedness.

Such arguments may seem persuasive — especially when presented as elegantly as they are by Piehl — but, in the end, I find them unconvincing. While it is true that Maurin provided a link to European Catholic thought, even Piehl admits that Dorothy Day was generally unaware of that rich legacy until Maurin introduced her to it — which is why his indoctrination began with giving her a "Catholic education." It is difficult, it seems to me, to pass off such a formative influence as merely symbolic. As for the need for a male front-man to appease hierarchical prejudice against women in leadership, Piehl ignores the venerable Catholic custom of female founders of lay communities and institutions. Finally, while Peter may have fit Dorothy Day's notions of sanctity, his symbolic usefulness with the more conventionally pious seems questionable given the decidedly mixed reviews he got when sent out to proclaim the movement's message. Catholic Workers to this day delight in retelling the stories of Maurin's adventures on the lecture circuit: being mistaken for a plumber and sent to a rectory basement to fix the pipes, being overlooked as a "bum" in a train station by his welcoming party, being thrown out of a Knights of Columbus meeting. On one occasion, a priest who had invited Maurin to address a parish discussion group demanded a refund of the car fare he'd advanced on the ground that he'd been promised a scholar, not a derelict. If Day was looking for a figure of saintly character acceptable to mainstream Catholic expectations, she could have done better than Maurin.

In support of his position that Day to some extent, whether consciously or unconsciously, created the Maurin "legend," Piehl also cites a number of instances in which she ignored Maurin's opinions when they were contrary to her own. Peter wanted the paper to be called *The Catholic Radical,* for example; Dorothy insisted on *The Catholic Worker* (one can almost see Maurin's Gallic shrug as he reacted to this defeat with "man proposes, woman disposes"). Further, Maurin initially contemplated that Catholic Worker houses of hospitality would serve only males; he proposed at one point broadcasting his Easy Essays over loudspeakers in public places; and he suggested that the Worker send out bands of youthful "Troubadours for Christ" who would sing his message on street corners. Piehl catches something of the reality of Dorothy's complex relationship with Maurin when he cites a letter in which she insists to an overeager correspondent that she and the Worker don't need to hear about any more of Peter's new ideas, thank you, as they are quite busy enough trying to put into practice the ideas he's already given them. There was also the matter of Day's support of organized labor in the face of Maurin's misgivings about such divisive strategies for social change.

While it is true that Day vetoed or ignored some of Maurin's more extravagant proposals (just as she apparently suppressed some of his pronouncements which she felt would needlessly antagonize the episcopacy), when it came to fundamentals she proved remarkably willing to have her opinions molded, albeit sometimes gradually, by his views. Even on the matter of organized labor, after World War II, as Robert Ellsberg points out, *The Catholic Worker* devoted remarkably little space to labor news, apart from consistent support for Cesar Chavez and the United Farm Workers. (The U.F.W., in Day's view, merited such attention by virtue of its unabashedly Catholic spirit and its embrace of the methods of Gandhian nonviolence.) Further, despite her advocacy of unions in principle, Day could be severely critical of labor leadership. In one of several examples of such criticism, she wrote in 1936 — using words strongly reflecting Maurin's views — that the "better conditions" for workers which labor seeks are finally only a "means to [a spiritual] end. But the labor movement has lost sight of this fact. The leaders have forgotten such a thing as a philosophy of labor. They have not given the worker the philosophy of labor, and they have betrayed him."

Piehl also raises the interesting question as to whether what he terms Maurin's "romantic medievalism" — his rejection of cities, capitalism and technology in favor of a simpler society held together by the church — means that Maurin was fundamentally nothing more than a reactionary. If so, one would presumably need to look to Dorothy Day for those elements of Worker thought that make the movement worthy of continuing consideration.

Of course, simply characterizing certain elements of Maurin's teaching as "reactionary" or "romantic" sidesteps a vital question: What if, however one labels such ideas, they happen to be *true*? Concerns over purportedly reactionary elements in Maurin's thought in many cases probably say more about the philosophical biases of those who express them than they do about the Worker vision itself.

Most of those drawn to the Catholic Worker tend toward the perspective and sympathies of the left. The *National Catholic Reporter* has often covered the movement; Catholics United for the Faith has not been known to express much interest in it. Dorothy Day is a popular figure among liberal Catholics; her life and witness provoke little enthusiasm among conservatives in the Church. The irony is that, in certain (though far from all) of its convictions, the Catholic Worker — at least as it found expression through Maurin and Day — shares more common ground with traditionalist Catholics than it does with that progressive wing of the Church which now holds the movement in such esteem. This does not mean, contrary to charges occasionally leveled against it, that the Worker is philosophically inconsistent. The Catholic Worker simply has what Dorothy Day in her later years, quoting John XXIII, liked to call "concordances" with both right and left, concordances made possible by virtue of the fact that it ultimately takes its stand outside both.

Maurin himself did say "My word is tradition. I am a radical of the right." He also often insisted that his philosophy was "not a new philosophy but a very old philosophy, a philosophy so old that it looks like new." Yet — at least in its broader outlines — the whole of the Worker idea is given voice in Maurin's "Essays," not just its arguably reactionary elements. Further, if the substance of the Worker vision is to be attributed to Dorothy Day, it is remarkable how little of either that vision or the program for action based upon it has precedent in her background or prior beliefs. True, as Robert Coles notes in

Dorothy Day: A Radical Devotion, Maurin's teaching "fell on fertile ground." Day undoubtedly had a genuine empathy for the poor. She burned with righteous anger over the injustices of a system that kept so many in poverty and longed to find a way to change that system. As she later wrote in *Loaves and Fishes*, one of her several autobiographical works:

> I had a very definite point of view about poverty, unemployment, and my own vocation to try to do something about it all. ... So, when Peter began talking about what "we need," it sounded clear and logical.

Nevertheless, before encountering Maurin, Day was, as she wrote to her student correspondent, "far better at making a criticism of the social order than ... offering any constructive ideas in relation to it."

In the end, my own view that Maurin is the ultimate source of the Worker vision — for all Dorothy Day's contributions to the working out of that vision and all her witness to its enduring power — is based on one relatively simple observation: For five years after her conversion, Day had floundered, finding no way within the context of her new Catholic identity to act upon her long-standing commitment to the cause of the poor and the workers. Six months after meeting Peter Maurin, she was a dramatically changed person, striking out on a unique and difficult path to which she remained faithful for the rest of her long life. However much her own history and personality may have contributed to this vocation, they were apparently not enough to create it. Something remarkable happened to her. I see no reason to look further than the event which she herself always cited to explain the change: God sent her Peter Maurin.

Most of us, perhaps understandably, are more comfortable with Dorothy Day than we are with Peter Maurin and his sometimes eccentric notions and sing-song essays. Her personality, her passion, even her sins are more appealing to us than Peter's idiosyncratic holiness. Maurin himself seems to have understood something of the difficulty he posed:

> They say that I am crazy
> because I refuse to be crazy
> the way everyone else is crazy.

If reality is what the Gospel and Christian tradition proclaim it to be, if self-emptying love is the source of all that is and if such love will be the "measure of all things," then the civilization we have created ("the way everyone else is crazy") is crazy indeed. Crazy for its indifference to those things that truly matter, crazy for its casual and premeditated cruelties, crazy for its smug certainty that its own "pragmatic realism" is a better gauge of truth than the "romantic idealism" of a prophet like Peter Maurin with his dirty clothes and funny accent, calling us to turn back the juggernaut of our much-vaunted "progress." Conversely, if the values and implied faith of the world we inhabit represent sanity, then it is sanctity that is "crazy" and those who would follow the way of Christ have no choice but to be holy fools.

When possessions and power and sensual self-indulgence are everywhere celebrated as the highest human goods, it is nothing short of folly to embrace a life informed by a determination to, as Maurin put it:

... foster a society
based on creed
instead of greed,
on systematic unselfishness
instead of systematic selfishness,
on gentle personalism
instead of rugged individualism. ...

But if the Gospel is true, such holy folly, such "craziness," would seem the only sort of life worth striving for, the "pearl of great price" for which we would sell everything we call our own.

The form such divine folly must take is surely different for every person. As Maurin wrote in an editorial in the second issue of *The Catholic Worker* in June of 1933: "I am not saying that my program is for everyone. It is for those who choose to embrace it." Yet before we too quickly breathe a sigh of relief that we are off the hook, that the life adopted by Maurin, Day and the Worker is only for the extraordinary few, the saints and revolutionaries, not for ordinary people like us, we might do well to remember that the Gospel insists that each one of us is intended to be nothing less than a saint.

We may not all be called to be Catholic Workers, as Maurin himself wrote. Yet surely we must each seriously confront the fundamental issues that the *fact* of the Worker and its witness pose for us.

The extraordinary Russian nun and seer, Mother Macaria, who died in 1993, is remembered by her biographer as lamenting how careless we are about our lives, how little we do toward the salvation our own souls or the redemption of our world. Peter Maurin's vision refuses to let us rest comfortably in such carelessness. Dorothy Day's life "on pilgrimage" gives compelling testimony to the necessity of accepting active responsibility for the transformation of all things through our own choice to follow Christ and take up the "folly of the cross."

Whatever the specifics of our immediate response, respond we must. As Dorothy Day wrote in 1957, reflecting on time she had spent in jail that year for once again protesting New York's civil defense drills:

> We can be responsible only for the one action of the present moment. But we can beg for an increase of love in our hearts that will vitalize and transform these actions ... know[ing] that God will take them and multiply them, as Jesus multiplied the loaves and fishes.

This any one of us can do. This we must do if we are to be fully human. The personalist revolution — and through it, the remaking and healing of all that is — is made up of just such actions. And, Ammon Hennacy would remind us in that irritating way of his, there are no excuses for waiting. We can begin right now.

Made in the USA
Middletown, DE
21 June 2020